GOLDSMITHS' COLLEGE

Her Royal Highness the Princess Royal, Chancellor of the University of London, signed the College Visitors' Book on 2 November 1988, on her first visit to Goldsmiths'.

A. E. Firth

Goldsmiths' College

A Centenary Account

THE ATHLONE PRESS
London & Atlantic Highlands, NJ

First published 1991 by The Athlone Press Ltd
1 Park Drive, London NW11 7SG
and 171 First Avenue, Atlantic Highlands, NJ 07716

British Library Cataloguing-in-Publication Data
Firth, A. E. (Anthony E.)
Goldsmiths' College: a centenary account.
1. London. Universities, history
I. Title
378.42163

ISBN 0 485 11384 8
ISBN 0 485 12072 0 pbk

Library of Congress Cataloging-in-Publication Data
Firth, A. E. (Anthony E.)
Goldsmiths' College: a centenary account / A. E. Firth.
p.   cm.
Includes bibliographical references (p.   ) and index.
ISBN 0 485 11384 8. – ISBN 0 485 12072 0 (pbk.)
1. Goldsmiths' College – History. I. Title.
LF419.5.G6F57 1991
378.421'6 – dc20

Produced for the publishers by
John Taylor Book Ventures

Designed by Alan Bartram
Typeset by Ronset Ltd, Darwen, Lancashire
Made and printed in Great Britain by
BAS Printers Ltd, Over Wallop, Stockbridge, Hampshire

Contents

Foreword

I have been privileged to serve as Warden of Goldsmiths' at a crucial period of the College's history, and I am delighted by the spirit and determination with which it is preparing to embark on the second century of its existence.

Its fortunes over its first hundred years are recorded in this volume; and the College is much indebted to its former Deputy Warden, Mr A. E. Firth, for the verve and assiduity he has brought to the compilation of its history. Our thanks are also due to Knox Cropper, Chartered Accountants, the College's auditors since 1905, to the Goldsmiths' Company and to an anonymous benefactor, who have generously helped to defray the costs of publication.

As the present history records, the College has gone through some difficult times, beset as it has been by anxieties about its constitutional status, its financial prospects, its survival as an independent institution, and even its continuance as part of London University. But throughout these years of uncertainty, staff have remained dedicated and resilient, and unwavering in their belief in Goldsmiths' manifest destiny as a University presence in South-east London. Its admission as a full School of London University in August 1988 was the fulfilment of the intentions of the Goldsmiths' Company when they presented the College they had founded to the University, and the fulfilment also of the aspirations of the College itself over very many years.

Many people contributed to this great development, but special mention must be made of two of my predecessors as Warden, Sir Ross Chesterman and Dr Richard Hoggart; two successive Vice-Chancellors, Professor Sir Randolph Quirk and Lord Flowers; the Principal of the University, Mr Peter Holwell; Mr William McCall, a lay member of the University Court who played a crucial role; Sir Charles Carter, Chairman of the College Delegacy and then of Council; and senior academic and administrative colleagues – in particular the Secretary, Mr Shane Guy, the Finance Officer, Mr Barry Tait, Mr Firth himself, the Deans, Dr Doreen Asso, Mr Peter Cresswell, Professor A. V. Kelly, Dr Marion Kimberley and the late Professor Alan Little, and the Director of Continuing Education, Mr Malcolm Barry. But equally important has been the firm resolution of the Academic Board and Governing Body of the College, and the support of the academic community as a whole – both staff and students – which I have valued in good times and bad. It says much for the morale and spirit of the College that it has been able to take very difficult decisions and carry them through without internal strife or divisions, and that it has consistently pursued its academic objectives regardless of the hazards, difficulties and uncertainties so frequently created for it by external agencies.

Particularly gratifying were the terms on which Goldsmiths' change of status was finally approved – that the College should not seek (as it had occasionally been tempted to do) to become a carbon copy of other Schools of the University, but that it should preserve and develop its distinctive features, building on existing strengths. These include the College's special relationship with its local community (unique in London University terms); the provision of part-time as well as full-time degree, diploma and certificate courses; an extensive programme of continuing education and access courses; the development of the creative and performing arts at a high level of excellence along with the traditional humanities; the combination in the social sciences of academic distinction with the application of each discipline to the problems of inner city areas like that in which the College is itself located; the contribution of education to debates on current policy, new curricular developments, and the training of teachers for inner city schools; and the mingling on campus of students recruited nationally, internationally, and locally.

The mixture is a rich one. The vitality of the College is unmistakable. It is moving resolutely into the future, in spite of dire financial cuts now being imposed on it by the recently established Universities Funding Council. (*'Nescis, mi fili, quantula sapientia homines regantur.'*) I am proud to have been associated with such a vigorous, dynamic and innovative institution.

Long may it flourish.

Andrew Rutherford

Introduction

This little book has been written as a contribution to the centenary celebrations planned by Goldsmiths' College for 1991. It is not a full scholarly history; it is intended simply to tell the story of the College up to the present time and to try to show how and why it developed into the singular institution it now is. Its academic, legal and constitutional position has always been odd; 'Byzantine complexity' has been a phrase often used in descriptions of it. As will appear, the College has been subject to the advice, the inspection and, in varying degrees, the control of a great number of external academic and official bodies. But as few subjects are less appealing than the records of long-concluded negotiations, accounts of the dealings between the College and these external authorities have been kept as brief as, it is hoped, is compatible with clarity.

The Author has listed in Appendix C those who have generously helped him in various ways. But he is, of course, wholly responsible for any errors, omissions or misjudgements.

The experience of the last hundred years suggests that it would not be wise to prophesy how the next hundred will turn out. So, in wishing the College and all its members well, the Author has decided to use the ancient, but safely unspecific, monastic salutation: 'Ad Multos Annos'.

Part One

1 Toll-gate at New Cross 1763.

2 View of New Cross 1770.

1 New Cross in the Nineteenth Century

3 A gentleman's residence in nineteenth-century New Cross.

In 1789, a Deptford distiller called William Goodhew built himself a house in New Cross on the site now occupied by the main building of the College. It must have been a pleasant enough spot. The great outward expansion of London had hardly begun and between Southwark and Bermondsey to the west and the ancient borough of Deptford to the east, a broad tract of land ran southwards from the marshes of Rotherhithe to the wooded hills of Lewisham. It was an area of small hamlets and farmsteads and fine gentlemen's residences, and, especially, of market gardens, for the soil was richly fertile and the City's appetite for its products voracious.

Almost fifty years later, Mr Goodhew's house was knocked down, to be replaced by the Royal Naval School. Even by then, the scene was changing. The roads from the City to the south-east had been greatly improved by the New Cross Turnpike Trust; regular omnibus services were under way; and the great middle-class migration to the leafy suburbs was beginning. The process was greatly accelerated by the building of new bridges across the Thames and, above all, by the coming of the railways. The very first London railway, from Spa Road to Deptford, was opened in 1836 and, in the 1840s – the years of the 'Railway Mania' – the huge extensions down towards the Kent and Sussex coasts were embarked on.

These improvements in transport and communications were

4

4 A view of the London and Croydon Railway. The Counter Hill Academy can be discerned on the centre right of the print.

5 Houses under the railway near Deptford, from a wood engraving.

5

probably the decisive factors in the creation of the new suburbs. But the southern-moving emigrants from the city sought the more salubrious air of the Kent and Surrey hills, and the lower-lying areas near the river rapidly became heavily industrialised. Deptford had been in decline with the closing of its docks and shipyards after the Napoleonic wars, and New Cross was much affected by the railways. The fierce competition between rival companies, seeking to capture the lucrative traffic to the coasts, furnished the district with two stations barely a quarter of a mile apart, and an

6

7

8

6 A view from a modern hall of residence, Warmington Tower, which gives a good impression of part of the New Cross railway system.

7 St James's Hatcham in the 1870s. Serious disturbances took place in protest at the supposedly papistical practices of the incumbent, the Reverend Arthur Tooth.

8 Nineteenth-century housing opposite the College across Lewisham Way; and tree pruning.

extraordinary proliferation of parallel and intersecting railway tracks known as the New Cross Tangle. There followed marshalling yards, workshops, engine-sheds and mean houses for the railway workers. New railway-related industrial concerns sprang up, most notably perhaps the Hatcham Iron Works, at which were produced some of the most famous locomotives of the age. When the Iron Works closed in 1872, part of the premises were used for the manufacture of Eno's Fruit Salts, an enterprise which was carried on at New Cross until as late as 1940. Steadily the farmers

9

9 The Marquis of Granby
public house. The present
building was erected in 1868.

10 Deptford Town Hall, an
exuberant Edwardian building
constructed between 1902 and
1907 to designs by the
prominent firm of Lanchester,
Stewart and Rickards.

and market gardeners sold up and the larger landowners, like the
Haberdashers' Company, made their acres over for development.
The huge brick-fields lying immediately to the south of the
College were built over in the 1850s and 1860s. By 1870, the whole
area had become urbanised and there was very little open space
left between Deptford and Southwark. Only the activities of the
Luftwaffe in the Second World War have made any significant
differences to the street pattern thus established.

The church, it must be said, was quicker than the state to take
note of these demographic changes. In 1847, a new parish – St
James's, Hatcham – was carved out of the large parish of St Paul's,
Deptford, its rather charmless church being built immediately to
the north of the College between 1849 and 1854. It lay then within
the diocese of Rochester. New Cross itself was never an
administrative area, being a rather ill-defined region which took
its name from an ancient hostelry and stage-post called the
Golden Cross. Indeed, until the end of the nineteenth century,
when the counties were forced to withdraw their frontiers in the
face of the inexorable advance of London, it lay partly in the
hundred of Brixton in the county of Surrey, and partly in the
hundred of Blackheath in the county of Kent, the county boundary
actually passing between what are now the main buildings of the
College and the Theatre and running diagonally across the back
field. New Cross was absorbed in 1902 into the borough of
Deptford, which in 1965 was itself merged with the London
borough of Lewisham.

11 The Counter Hill Academy.

2 The Counter Hill Academy and the Royal Naval School

12 View of the Royal Naval School, built between 1843 and 1845 to the designs of John Shaw (1803-70).

William Goodhew unluckily died shortly after he had moved into his fine new house, and from 1792 until it was demolished in 1838 it housed the school known as the Counter Hill Academy, run by three generations of the Bentley family. The site was then acquired by the Royal Naval School, a boarding school for the sons of officers in the Royal Navy and the Royal Marines, founded in 1833 and originally located in Camberwell. The foundation stone of the new building was laid by Prince Albert on 1 July 1843, and within a few months staff and pupils had moved into their new quarters.

The Naval School remained at New Cross until 1889, when it removed itself to a more rural site at Mottingham. From then on it declined steadily, had its royal patronage withdrawn, and finally closed in 1910. In its heyday it had enjoyed powerful royal and aristocratic support. Queen Victoria regularly contributed £100 per year to its funds, Prince Leopold distributed prizes on at least one occasion, the Duke of Northumberland was one of its lordly patrons, and several admirals sat on its governing body. All the same, it suffered from a number of disadvantages. Its aim being to provide sound and cheap education for the sons of 'less affluent naval and marine officers', it often found it necessary to reduce, or even remit altogether, the fees it charged. In 1851, for instance, only fourteen pupils out of a total of 176 were paying the full fees of £50.

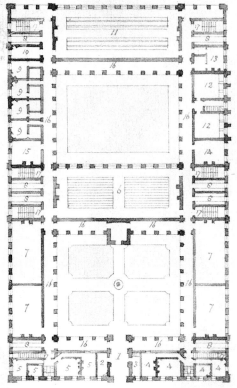
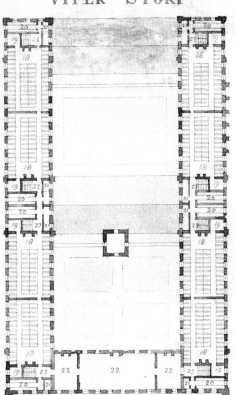

GROVND · PLAN   VPPER · STORY

REFERENCE

1. Entrance
2. Receiving Room
3. Porter's Lodge
4. Head Master's House
5. Secretary's House
6. School
7. Class Rooms
8. Lavatorys
9. Under Masters Rooms
10. D° Dining Room
11. Hall
12. Kitchens & Offices

13. Matrons Rooms
14. Women Servants Room
15. Men Servants room
16. Arcades
17. Staircases
18. Dormitorys
19. Ushers Rooms
20. Wardrobes
21. Water Closets
22. Library & Museum
23. Staircases
NB The Bedrooms of the
Officers are provided on a
Mezzanine Floor

ROYAL · NAVAL · SCHOOL

13 Ground plan of the Royal
Naval School.

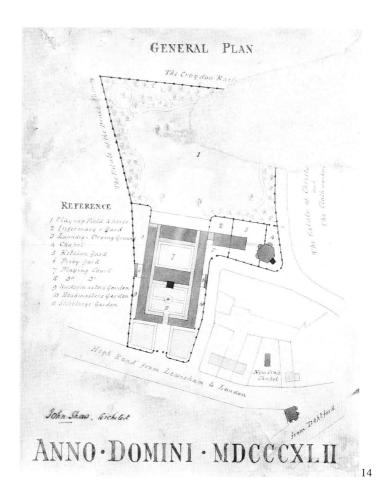

GENERAL PLAN

The Croydon Rail

REFERENCE
1 Playing Field 4 Acres
2 Infirmary 4 Yard
3 Laundry & Drying Ground
4 Chapel
5 Kitchen Yard
6 Privy Yard
7 Playing Court
8 Do   Do
9 Undermasters Garden
10 Headmasters Garden
11 Secretarys Garden

High Road from Lewisham to London

New Cross Chapel

John Shaw Architect

from Deptford

ANNO·DOMINI·MDCCCXLII

14

14 Site plan of the Royal Naval School.

15 The quadrangle of the Royal Naval School as illustrated in the *Pictorial Times* of 15 February 1845.

15

16

17

They were all the sons of civilians; officers' sons were charged anything from nothing to £31. This meant that the school was engaged in a constant struggle to obtain donations and bene-factions, in order to keep itself in being. Also, as has been shown, New Cross was becoming an increasingly improbable location for a public school. Other famous London schools faced the same problem. Charterhouse moved out to Surrey in 1872, St Paul's to Hammersmith in 1884, and Christ's Hospital to Horsham in 1902. Quite a number of independent schools were set up in the nineteenth century to provide a reasonably cheap education for the sons of particular professional groups; Epsom College, for example, catered especially for the sons of doctors, and Haileybury was established by the Directors of the East India Company for servants of the company itself. Not all such establishments survived but those that did managed to broaden their appeal and find themselves a place in the general public school system. The Naval School did not succeed in developing in that way and so found itself without a useful function.

16 The tower and cupola over the school room.

17 Tram crews at New Cross Gate Station, *c*.1900.

18 The post near the College tennis courts, marking the old boundary between Kent and Surrey.

18

19 The commemorative card
for the opening of the
Goldsmiths' Company's
Technical and Recreative
Institute.

3 The Goldsmiths' Institute

Once the Royal Naval School had decided to move, it sold its New Cross property to one of the great City Livery Companies, the Worshipful Company of Goldsmiths, for £25,000. The buildings were re-opened on the 22 July 1891 by the Prince of Wales as the Goldsmiths' Company's Technical and Recreative Institute.

The Institute came into being for two main reasons. Firstly, the City of London Parochial Charities Act of 1883 had freed many civic funds from what had often become unworkable restrictions, and enabled the charity commissioners to authorise their use for more appropriate purposes. Secondly, there were strong public and parliamentary feelings that Britain was falling behind other countries, particularly Germany, in the provision of cheap scientific and technical education. This resulted in the passing of the Technical Instruction Act of 1889. A plan was then drawn up by which the charity commissioners would provide £150,000 towards the establishment of three polytechnics in south London, provided an equal sum was raised from private sources. However, the Goldsmiths' Company, one of the richest of the livery companies, decided to provide one of these institutions at its own charge: hence the Goldsmiths' Institute.

The opening ceremony was quite an occasion. The prince was accompanied by the princess; present were members of the court and the livery of the company, peers and members of the House of Commons, representatives of local authorities, justices of the peace, clergy, local businessmen, and the like. The whole gathering was entertained by a cantata specially composed by Churchill Sibley, organist to the Institute, set to what one newspaper charitably described as 'dainty verses' written by H. Sutherland Edwards. Appropriate speeches were made and the prince and princess made a tour of the buildings.

Then the Institute got down to work. Its object was 'the promotion of the individual skill, general knowledge, health and well being of young men and women belonging to the industrial, working and poorer classes'. The Institute's handbook for 1896-7 shows how fully this object had, by then, been achieved. Instruction was being given in the whole range of subjects or areas listed in illustration no. 22 (page 27).

Examinations were conducted at the end of each session, and certificates and prizes awarded by the City and Guilds of London

20

20 The front of the Institute building, *c.* 1891.

21 The site plan of the Institute.

22 The subjects taught at the Institute, as listed in the handbook for 1896-7.

Institute, the government's Science and Art Department, and the Society of Arts. On 9 December 1896, Augustine Birrell, the future Liberal cabinet minister, distributed prizes and certificates to 614 young people and by 1900 the total number of enrolled students had topped 7000. Instruction was also given for London University pass degrees in Science; and University Extension Courses were held. Course fees for a whole year ranged from three shillings to fifteen shillings; and the Company itself offered scholarships worth five or ten pounds to boys and girls who had attended public elementary schools in the Greenwich School Board division.

The recreative and social side of the Institute's work was just as successful. For those who attended classes, membership cost, per annum, seven shillings for men and five shillings for women. The principal advantages of membership were described as being 'the use of the library, reading, writing and locker rooms, two recreation grounds, a cinder running track and a large swimming bath'. Organ recitals were free and admission charges for concerts reduced. There were temperance refreshment rooms at popular prices, two gymnasia, meeting rooms for clubs and societies, and

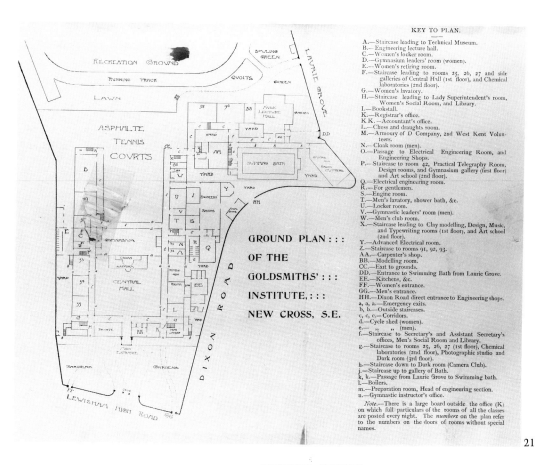

GROUND PLAN : : :

OF THE

GOLDSMITHS' : : :

INSTITUTE, : : :

NEW CROSS, S.E.

KEY TO PLAN.

A.—Staircase leading to Technical Museum.
B.—Engineering lecture hall.
C.—Women's locker room.
D.—Gymnasium leaders' room (women).
E.—Women's retiring room.
F.—Staircase leading to rooms 25, 26, 27 and side galleries of Central Hall (1st floor), and Chemical laboratories (2nd floor).
G.—Women's lavatory.
H.—Staircase leading to Lady Superintendent's room, Women's Social Room, and Library.
I.—Bookstall.
K.—Registrar's office.
K K.—Accountant's office.
L.—Chess and draughts room.
M.—Armoury of D Company, 2nd West Kent Volunteers.
N.—Cloak room (men).
O.—Passage to Electrical Engineering Room, and Engineering Shops.
P.—Staircase to room 42, Practical Telegraphy Room, Design rooms, and Gymnasium gallery (first floor) and Art school (2nd floor).
Q.—Electrical engineering room.
R.—For gentlemen.
S.—Engine room.
T.—Men's lavatory, shower bath, &c.
U.—Locker room.
V.—Gymnastic leaders' room (men).
W.—Men's club room.
X.—Staircase leading to Clay modelling, Design, Music, and Typewriting rooms (1st floor), and Art school (2nd floor).
Y.—Advanced Electrical room.
Z.—Staircase to rooms 91, 92, 93.
A A.—Carpenter's shop.
B B.—Modelling room.
C C.—Exit to grounds.
D D.—Entrance to Swimming Bath from Laurie Grove.
E E.—Kitchens, &c.
F F.—Women's entrance.
G G.—Men's entrance.
H H.—Dixon Road direct entrance to Engineering shops.
a, a, a.—Emergency exits.
b, b.—Outside staircases.
c, c, c.—Corridors.
d.—Cycle shed (women).
e.— „ „ (men).
f.—Staircase to Secretary's and Assistant Secretary's offices, Men's Social Room and Library.
g.—Staircase to rooms 25, 26, 27 (1st floor), Chemical laboratories (2nd floor), Photographic studio and Dark room (3rd floor).
h.—Staircase down to Dark room (Camera Club).
j.—Staircase up to gallery of Bath.
k, k.—Passage from Laurie Grove to Swimming bath.
l.—Boilers.
m.—Preparation room, Head of engineering section.
n.—Gymnastic instructor's office.

Note.—There is a large board outside the office (K) on which full particulars of the rooms of all the classes are posted every night. The *numbers* on the plan refer to the numbers on the doors of rooms without special names.

21

SUBJECTS TAUGHT.

Ambulance.	French.	Orchestra, Institute.
Applied Mechanics.	Gas Manufacture.	Orchestral Classes.
Arithmetic.	Geometry, Plane and Solid.	Pattern Making.
Art.	German.	Photography.
Art Needlework.	Grammar and Analysis.	Physics, Practical & Theoretical.
Book Illustration.	Guitar.	Physiology, Human.
Bookkeeping.	Gymnastics.	Piano.
Botany.	Handwriting.	Plumbing.
Brick Cutting.	Harmony and Theory of Music.	Repoussé.
Brickwork.	Heat.	Sewing, Plain.
Building Construction.	Hygiene.	Shorthand.
Carpentry.	Laundry Work.	Singing, Choral.
Chemistry.	Light.	Ditto Solo.
Choir, Institute.	London University, Matriculation	Ditto Institute Choir.
Choral Singing.	and Intermediate B.Sc. Preparation.	Smithing.
Civil Service.	paration.	Sound, Light and Heat.
Clay Modelling.	Machine Drawing.	Spanish.
Commercial Training.	Magnetism and Electricity.	Steam and Heat Engines.
Cookery.	Mandoline.	Swimming.
Design.	Mathematics.	Tailors' Cutting.
Drawing from Nude.	Mechanics Applied.	Telegraphy, Practical.
Dressmaking and Cutting.	Ditto Theoretical.	Typewriting.
Engineering, Electrical.	Millinery.	Typography.
Engineering, Mechanical.	Modelling.	University Extension Lectures.
English Composition.	Music.	Violin.
Fitting and Machining.	Oils and Fats (Chemistry applied	Wood Carving.
Flute.	to).	Zither.

NEW CLASSES.—If a sufficient number of intending students signify their desire to join any specific class not on the time table as at present issued, the Governors will consider the desirability of forming such a class.

NOTE.—The arrangements detailed in this Handbook are subject to alteration and addition as the Governors may from time to time direct.

Artisans, handicraftsmen and apprentices are admitted at half fees to classes specially applicable to their trade, if application is made each year before the Class Session commences in October.

All suggestions and complaints should be officially addressed to the Secretary of the Goldsmiths' Company's Institute.

A CHEMISTRY STUDENT

23 A chemistry student as illustrated in the 1896-7 handbook.

ample sports facilities. In 1896, the following clubs and societies were functioning:

Athletic Club	Cricket Club
Art Club	Cycling Club
Choir	Camera Club
Engineering Society	Swimming Club
French Society	Tennis Club
Chess and Draughts Club	Shorthand Society
Chemistry Society	Rugby Football Club
Rowing Club	Boxing Club
Ramblers' Club	Women's Tennis Club
Voluntary Stewards' Association	Women's Ramblers' Club
Men's Literary Society	Women's Chess, Draughts
Quoits and Bowls Club	and Halma Club

Women's Literary Society

Many of these were extremely active and well provided for. In 1895-6, the choir and orchestra performed *Messiah*, the *Creation*, *Elijah* and the *Golden Legend*; the Quoits and Bowls Club had its own bowling ground and two quoits pitches; the Cricket Club fielded four XIs every Saturday and went on a country tour each August; and the Women's Tennis Club had three grass and four asphalt courts.

The day-to-day running of the Institute was the responsibility of

24 Modelling from life at the Institute.

the Secretary, an Oxford-educated barrister named J. S. Redmayne. By 1903 he had under him a total staff of more than 150, of whom about 40 were full-time employees. The Governing Body consisted of the Prime Warden and Wardens of the Company, seven members of its court and six co-opted members. Between 1889 and 1904, the Company spent almost £300,000 on the Institute, and it seems clear that this was money well spent, as the Institute certainly met urgent educational and social needs. It is ironic that so successful a venture should have come to an end as a direct result of Balfour's famous Education Act of 1902 and the subsequent London Education Act.

What happened was this. On 12 February 1903, Sir Walter Prideaux, the Company's Clerk, circulated to members of the court a memorandum in which he proposed that the Company should close its Institute in 1904, offer it, as a going concern, to the Education Authority for London, and devote the monies thus saved to other educational work. His reasons for making these proposals were that, in the future, the London County Council would have 'supreme power' over all educational institutions in London. It would be desirable for the Institute to be included in any general scheme, but he felt sure that the Company would not wish an institution which it ran to be subject 'to the inspection and control of another body'. He did not think that, in the long run, the Company could successfully compete with institutions

25

25 A cookery class at the
Institute.

26 A building class at the
Institute.

27 Sir Arthur Rücker, the first
Principal of the University of
London 1901-8.

28 Sir Walter Prideaux, clerk to
the Worshipful Company of
Goldsmiths' 1882-1918,
member of the College
Delegacy 1904-11.

funded out of the rates, and 'the relief of the rates was not the
object of the court when they founded their institution'. On 11
March the court agreed to Prideaux's proposals and authorised
him to find out whether the Technical Education Board of the
LCC would accept the Institute as a gift, and undertake its
management.

It does not appear, however, than any such approach was ever
made to the LCC. Instead, during the summer and autumn, Sir
Walter entered into negotiations with Sir Arthur Rücker, the
Principal of London University. At first, the idea was that the New
Cross Institute might become part of a new Institute of Applied
Science, which there was talk of founding within the University.
Later, however, the idea developed that the buildings should be
used to house a Teacher Training College. On 29 February 1904, a
formal offer of the gift of the Institute was made to the University,
the only condition being that the buildings should always be used
for educational purposes. The Senate accepted the offer in April of
that year.

26

27

28

29 The Goldsmiths' Hall, in a watercolour by Herbert Finn painted in 1913.

The Company's decision to offer its Institute to the University rather than to the LCC met with disapproval in some quarters. There were protests in the local Press. The Mayor of Deptford became much enraged and, in July 1905, the LCC passed, by sixty-five to thirty-five, what amounted to a vote of censure on the Company for having given up its work at New Cross. It does not seem to be possible to discover why Sir Walter's original plan of handing the whole thing over to the LCC was dropped, but the LCC had, at the time, a large progressive, that is to say, radical majority, and there is evidence in private letters written to Sir Walter that there was a certain amount of hostility to it within the Company. But it is not possible to say whether these feelings were decisive in Prideaux's sudden change of course.

4 The College Established

30 William Loring, the first Warden of the College 1905-15. The bust is by F. Halnon, who taught sculpture at the Institute and at the College.

Immediately after the Senate had accepted, in April 1904, the offer of the site and buildings of the Institute, together with fittings, apparatus and equipment, no fewer than three interlocking committees were established to plan the future of the new institution. They were the Goldsmiths' Institute Committee, the Goldsmiths' Institute Interim Management Committee and the Goldsmiths' Institute Interim Management Committee acting jointly with representatives of the LCC. This situation was tidied up in the autumn of 1904 with the appointment of a new Goldsmiths' College Delegacy, responsible to the University Senate, of which the membership was as follows:

8 members of the University Senate, nominated by the Senate
2 representatives of the LCC
1 representative of Kent County Council
1 representative of Surrey County Council
1 representative of Middlesex County Council
1 representative of Croydon Borough Council
2 representatives of the Goldsmiths' Company
The Principal of the University
The University Professor of Education

Sir Edward Busk, the then Vice-Chancellor, was the first Chairman of the Delegacy, a post he retained until 1919.

It had already been decided that the most appropriate use for the building would be to house a Teacher Training College, with the students taking the usual two-year Certificate of Education course. The University believed that local authorities in the London area would require education of a 'University' character for their teachers and that greater numbers of students would have to be provided for than the existing training colleges could cope with. Also, the idea had financial advantages. The University had very little money of its own, certainly none to spend at New Cross. A Training College would, in effect, be paid for by capitation grants from the Board of Education and fees paid by local authorities in respect of the students they sent there. Negotiations were entered into and, in due course, it was agreed that 183 places should be reserved for the LCC, 92 each for Kent, Surrey and Middlesex County Councils, and 39 for the Borough of Croydon.

31 Thomas Raymont, Men's
Vice-Principal 1905-15; Acting
Warden 1915-19, second
Warden of the College 1919-27.

32 Miss Caroline Graveson,
Women's Vice-Principal
1905-34.

Before the first students at the new Training College arrived
on 28 September 1905 – the 'aboriginals' as they were to call
themselves in the future – the first staff appointments had of
course been made. William Loring was the Warden, a former
Cambridge Classics don and archaeologist and, at the time of
his appointment, the Director of Education for the West Riding
of Yorkshire. The Women's Vice-Principal was Miss Caroline
Graveson, from Liverpool's Day Training College, and the first
men's Vice-Principal, Thomas Raymont, previously Professor
of Education at University College, Cardiff. Eight men, including a Sergeant-Major Shipp, and ten women, had also been
appointed. A year later, these totals had risen to fourteen and
thirteen respectively, though the Sergeant-Major had dropped
off the list. The College was formally opened by Lord Rosebery,
the Chancellor of the University, on 29 September 1905; the
Prime Warden of the Goldsmiths' Company handed him a
golden key to the College; and the fourth educational institution to be sited on Mr Goodhew's land set out on its new and
uncharted course.

Constitutionally, the new College was in an odd and anomalous position. Between 1905 and 1988 it was, amongst other
things, 'an Institution with Recognised Teachers'. Sidney
Webb, the founder of the London School of Economics, had
been greatly concerned to establish academic links between
London University and the London Polytechnics. The IRT
system meant that students studying at such independent
institutions could, nonetheless, read for London University
degrees provided they were taught by staff recognised by the
University as competent University teachers; but Goldsmiths'
College, far from being an independent institution, was
actually owned by the University and had no legal or constitutional independence. The University even had to sign leases
on its behalf. And there was another oddity. Besides the
Training Department, the College housed a number of other
activities which were, from 1905 onwards, paid for by means of
annual grants from the LCC: the School of Art, for example.
But the Delegacy could not maintain much in the way of direct
control over these activities as it did not pay for them, and
even the Warden was authorised to exercise only a general
supervision of them.

The Delegacy never forgot the Goldsmiths' Company's hope
that the College would one day become the University College
of south-east London, which would have involved a major
move into University degree work and a constitutional and
academic promotion to the status enjoyed by the great Colleges
and Schools of the University: such places as King's, or University College or the London School of Economics. In 1909, an

33 The Great Hall on 29 September 1905, the day on which the College was formally opened.

opportunity to pursue this object seemed to have arrived, with the appointment of a Royal Commission on the University under the chairmanship of Lord Haldane. The College Delegacy, in a submission to the Commission, proposed that the College should become in effect a centre for University education in south-east London, maintaining the Training Department and the School of Art but being allowed also to teach for undergraduate and postgraduate degrees as demand arose and to pursue research appropriate to a University institution. In this application, the College had considerable local support. In January 1911, the Mayor, Aldermen and Councillors of the metropolitan borough of Deptford submitted a memorial to the Senate of the University, the Haldane Commission, the LCC and the Goldsmiths' Company, praying that immediate steps be taken with a view to the establishment, in the near future, at the Goldsmiths' College in the Lewisham High Road, of a University College of south London, with low fees, available for evening as well as day classes. The memorial was courteous in tone but vigorous in purport. It recorded the view that 'prior to the time when the College was taken over from the Goldsmiths' Company it was of great service and importance to residents in Deptford and Lewisham, but by reason of their use as a Training College, its buildings are now of little value to the locality and as a matter of fact Deptford has less educational facilities now than it had ten years ago'.

34 The male staff 1905.

35 The female staff 1905.

36 Sports Day 1906. The Blomfield building was yet to be built.

37 Sir Edward Busk, first Chairman of the Delegacy 1904-19. Chairman of Convocation of the University of London 1892-1922, Vice Chancellor 1905-7.

34

35

But these representations were of no avail. The Haldane Commission in its interim report (1911) and in its final report (1913) took the view that the College should maintain its Training Department and its School of Art; that it should terminate all its other activities; and that its buildings should become the main centre for the London activities of the Workers' Educational Association. The Delegacy reacted angrily, almost incredulously, to these proposals, feeling that they amounted to a breach of the terms of the Goldsmiths' Company's original gift. At one point it made the interesting suggestion that King's College should quit its premises in the

36

37

Strand and re-establish itself at New Cross. But although many of the Haldane Commission's recommendations were overtaken by the war and never implemented, they were decisive for the immediate future of the College. On three separate occasions in the 1920s it raised the possibility of extending its degree work and becoming a School of the University. But it was not until after the Second World War that these possibilities were again really seriously discussed.

One of the reasons why the College wished to improve its constitutional position was a financial one. When Raymont retired from the Wardenship in 1927, he recorded that the College's history from 1905 to 1927 had been one long battle for financial survival. Most teacher training colleges were run by the churches, or by charitable trusts which had access to church funds. Local Authority colleges could be supported from the rates. In either case, the colleges could be provided with capital sums for building projects and the like. In the case of Goldsmiths' College, what was technically known as the 'providing authority' was the University of London. But the University had very little money of its own and, from 1919 onwards, when the University Grants Committee was established, University funds could only be made available for University purposes and the support of teacher training institutions was not regarded as a proper charge on them. So the College was constantly in difficulties. Student fees were paid by local authorities, and limited capitation grants were obtained from the Board of Education, but the College found it extremely difficult to raise money for major projects. An application to the University for a capital grant of just over £50,000 and a recurrent annual grant of £4,000 was firmly rejected in 1919. Just before the war, moreover, the LCC had

38 The inscription beneath the balustrade of the Blomfield building records the Goldsmiths' Company's benefaction, and reads:
UNIVERSITATIS LONDINIENSIS COLLEGIUM SOCIETATIS AURIFICUM MUNIFICENTIA INAUGURATUM A.D. MCMV AEDIFICIO NOVO EXORNATUM A.D. MCMVII.

insisted on a reduction in the fees charged to students and in 1913 had withdrawn from the arrangement by which it had undertaken to take up 183 student places in the College.

A near fatal crisis did occur during the First World War. Not surprisingly, the number of male students fell sharply, indeed to only fifteen by the last year of the war. In the 1915-6 session, the total number of students fell to its lowest level ever – 283. Various economies were made: the evening Science Department was finally closed in 1915, the academic staff offered to take a 15 per cent reduction in their salaries, the swimming bath was closed. A deficit on the catering account

39

39 Sports Day 1908, the Blomfield building having been completed.

40 New Cross before the motor-car.

40

was met by an emergency grant from the Goldsmiths' Company. The charge for the mid-day meal, which all students were required to take, was raised from 6d to 7d. Raymont assured the Delegacy that he felt that the students had been unnecessarily well fed and said he was determined that that should stop. 'Not only', he explained, 'the person responsible for buying the meat, but also the person who carves it, has had it impressed upon him that the College undertakes to provide a 7d meal and not a 9d one.'

Between 1905 and 1912 the Goldsmiths' Company had made an annual grant of £5,000 to the College, had made an addi-

41 First World War Roll of Honour.

tional special grant of £5,000 in 1905, and had financed the erection of the new School of Art building. But in 1910 the Company refused to extend its grant beyond 1912. It plainly felt, not unreasonably, that a financial crisis would inevitably occur unless the University could make a long-term plan for the College and it was affronted by the University's inability or unwillingness to provide any financial guarantees for its future. On 21 December 1910, Sir Walter Prideaux wrote:

In the absence of any statement on the part of the University showing a reasonable probability of permanence in the maintenance and development of Goldsmiths' College, the court does not feel able to consider the further renewal of the grant which the Company originally promised for a limited period and have since renewed until the year 1912.

In further correspondence he made it plain that, in the absence of any guaranteed funding from either the University or the LCC, the Company thought it right to say that it did not feel under any obligation 'to provide a College or University in south-east London and did not have the ability to undertake so large and indefinite an annual expense.' So, although the College rapidly established itself as one of the best training colleges in the country, its constitutional position remained uncertain and its solvency constantly in doubt.

5 The College Buildings

42 A perspective drawing of the School of Art building, designed by Sir Reginald Blomfield (1858-1942).

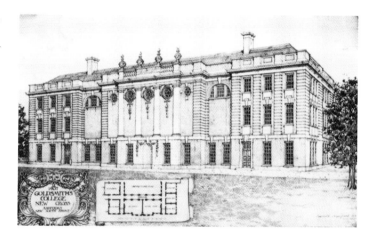

The buildings which the Goldsmiths' Company presented to the University had been erected for the Royal Naval School to the designs of John Shaw, at a cost of £35,000. Shaw was a highly competent architect, much admired by distinguished architectural historians such as Sir Nikolaus Pevsner, and H. S. Goodhart-Rendel, who believed that his buildings at New Cross displayed the first attempt in the nineteenth century to recapture something of the character of English architecture of the Wren period.

His design was basically a simple one; a rectangular shaped building fronting on to what is now Lewisham Way, with two long parallel wings stretching towards the south-west. Immediately behind the front of the building was an open, cloistered quadrangle, used in Naval School times as a parade-ground. This was closed off by a handsome building known as the 'school room', topped by a lantern and cupola. Behind was another quadrangle open to the school's playing fields.

Shaw's building was certainly unusual in that much public or semi-public building of the time was being done in Grecian or Gothic styles. Shaw's work, in red brick with stone facings and quoins, seems obviously to have owed something to Wren. The long fronts to the main buildings, with very little in the way of vertical articulation, certainly have similarities with Hampton Court.

43

44

43 Surrey Hostel in 1907. The   **44** The dining-room at Surrey
building was provided by the   House about 1907.
Surrey County Council.

45

46

45 Examinations in the Great Hall. The hall was created in 1891, when the old parade ground was roofed in to a design by J. W. Penfold. It makes an excellent concert hall.

46 Granville Park from a postcard dated 1907. Four houses were acquired in that year by Kent County Council for women students. Sir Arthur Rücker attended the opening ceremony conducted by Sir William Hart Dyke.

THE GROVE HOSTEL

(Temporary)

For Men

Inset—Study
at the
Grove Hostel

47

48

47 Grove Hall came into use as a men's hostel in 1912 and was sold in the 1980s to help finance the new Library building.

48 St Michael's Hostel was provided by the National Society for Church of England women students between 1907 and 1939.

49 The College Refectory before the First World War.

50 Pentland House in 1982. The building has been much extended since it was acquired for the College by the Goldsmiths' Company and opened as a hall of residence in 1913.

49

50

Considerable changes had been made to the buildings while the Goldsmiths' Company owned them. The old school room was converted into a gymnasium, the parade-ground roofed in by an exuberant feat of architectural engineering and turned into a concert hall, and a swimming pool built. The Chapel, formally deconsecrated by a private Act of Parliament, was refurbished as the main lecture room in 1892. (This building

51

51 Clyde House, later renamed Dean Hall, was, like Pentland House, provided for the College by the Goldsmiths' Company and opened in 1913.

52 The swimming bath, as illustrated in a College Guide published in 1917.

53 The tennis court, as illustrated in a College Guide published in 1917.

was possibly not designed by Shaw but it is, all the same, pleasingly reminiscent of one of Wren's less ambitious City churches.)

The Goldsmiths' Company, in the three years following the transfer of the Institute to the University, largely paid for a major new building closing off the second quadrangle on its south-western end. This was to house the College's School of Art and was built to the designs of Sir Reginald Blomfield. Blomfield was a prolific and competent architect of country houses and of official and semi-official buildings. He developed an almost obsessive hatred of modern architecture and had an immense admiration for Wren. His School of Art building for the College was a distinguished example of his work, though a good deal more monumental than anything Shaw had attempted. (Curiously, Blomfield is probably now best known for having, in the 1920s, advised the Central Electricity Board about the design of the standard form of electricity pylon.)

There have been no major changes to the appearance of the main block of College buildings since the completion of Blomfield's School of Art in 1908. There have been frequent minor re-arrangements of the room layout; new classrooms were built in the Blomfield quadrangle and, after a new building was erected in the 1960s to house two gymnasia, the former gym-

52

53

nasium – on the site of the old 'school room' – was converted
into refectories and common rooms, the refectory itself being
refurbished in 1983 in a mildly Moorish style. The swimming
pool was destroyed during the Second World War and never
rebuilt; the lantern and cupola over what had been the Chapel
were knocked off by an errant barrage-balloon and never replaced; and the finials which had adorned the main façades of
Shaw's buildings also disappeared during the war. The whole
roof of his building was destroyed by bombing, and the pitched
roof he had erected had to be replaced by a flat one, on account
of a post-war shortage of timber.

In 1968 it was discovered that the ornamental urns at the top
of the central pavilion of the Blomfield building had become
seriously corroded, and they had to be taken down. There was
some debate as to whether the College should try to obtain
funds to restore them. Mr R. E. Enthoven, whose firm,
Enthoven and Mock, had been responsible for some quite
extensive new building for the College in the 1960s, advised
against their restoration, on the grounds that the buildings his
firm had designed had been simple and economical in character
and outline, and inevitably contrasted strongly with the Blomfield grandeur. 'The removal of the urns does something to
reduce this lack of unity.' Sadly this advice had to be taken.

Perhaps as important as anything has been the great open
field which lies to the south-west of the main building, extended in 1927 by the purchase from the Railway Company of
the terraces at the far end, created when the railway-cutting
south of New Cross Gate station had been dug. This serves as a
sort of 'lung' for the College and its members, and its expanse
of lawns and trees constantly surprises visitors who reach the
College from the Old Kent Road or New Cross station.

54

55

56 The staff of the Training
Department 1918-19.

6 The Training Department to 1939

In 1944, a committee appointed by R. A. Butler, then President of the Board of Education, reported that 'the existing arrangements for the recognition, the training and the supply of teachers are chaotic'. This chaos was already developing apace by 1905. Broadly speaking, the training of teachers for work in public elementary schools took place in three sorts of institutions: small residential colleges provided mainly by the churches, day-training colleges provided since 1890 by many Universities and University Colleges, and a small number of colleges provided, following the Education Act of 1902, by local authorities. Syllabuses were devised, and examinations conducted, by the Board of Education, and some small degree of academic scrutiny was exercised by His Majesty's Inspectors. The standard course lasted for two years, leading to the award of a Certificate of Education. The Universities, however, quickly took themselves out of the system, preferring to provide for a one-year postgraduate course at the end of an ordinary three-year degree course. This happened, for instance, at the London Day Training College which by 1911 had become an almost entirely postgraduate institution. (In 1932 it was re-constituted as the University of London Institute of Education.)

Goldsmiths' College was therefore in this, as in many other ways, a unique institution. Not only was it, with the arrival of the second student entry in 1906, the largest teacher training college in the kingdom, it was the only one maintained by a University for the purpose of teaching for a two-year Certificate of Education course. This course qualified students for employment in the public sector of elementary education.

In the early days, for the first fifteen years or so, it had really to perform two functions: it had to provide both professional training and a decent general education at something like the level aimed for in modern sixth forms or, at best, in the first year of university degree courses. The reason for this was that the public education system did not, until after the Education Act of 1902 and H. A. L. Fisher's reforms of 1918, provide for much in the way of post-elementary education. For most aspiring teachers, the main route into the profession was to stay on at their schools and, under the guidance of the head teachers, begin to do some teaching of younger pupils themselves, and then sit

57 Professor A. N. Whitehead,
second Chairman of the
Delegacy 1920-24, and eminent
philosopher. Sketch by Paul
Drury.

58 Arthur Edis Dean, third
Warden of the College 1927-50.

59 Miss Dorothy Dymes,
Women's Vice-Principal
1935-53.

for the Queen's (later King's) Scholarship examination, which could qualify them for entry to and financial support at a Teacher Training College. Such was the route followed by Thomas Raymont, the second Warden of the College. The snag was, obviously, that this system did not by any means guarantee that a young man or woman thus entering a Teacher Training College knew much about any academic subject. Consequently, the Training Colleges, under the supervision of the Board of Education, had to devise syllabuses which would not only, in crude terms, teach their students how to teach, but also teach them the subjects which they might find themselves actually teaching others. The syllabus of the two-year course at Goldsmiths' provides a characteristic example. For the academic year 1907-8, for example, the compulsory subjects comprised:

1 English Language and Literature, including an introduction to the study of Greek and Roman Classical Literature.
2 Elementary Mathematics (including Arithmetic).
3 Elementary Science (curiously, women students could skip Mathematics and Science in favour of a Modern Language provided Arithmetic was not omitted).
4 English History.
5 Geography.
6 (a) Manual Training (including Woodwork) for men.
   (b) Domestic Training (including Needlework) for women.
7 Nature-study (the course being arranged, as far as possible, with reference to the natural seasons).
8 Physical Training, viz:
   (1) Exercises suitable for Elementary Schools.
   (2) Gymnastics (for suitable students).
   (3) Swimming (for suitable students).
9 Drawing and Blackboard Drawing (including the preparation of sketch-maps, diagrams and rough drawings to illustrate lessons).
10 Music, viz:
   (1) Theory of Music.
   (2) Singing and Voice Management.
11 Teaching, viz:
   (1) Theory and History.
   (2) Practice.
   (3) School Hygiene and elements of General Hygiene.

Students might also take a course in Scripture of an undenominational and academic kind, it being laid down that this course was voluntary on the part both of teachers and of students. In the second year, a student could also take two optional subjects, drawn from a list comprising French,

57

58

59

German, Hebrew and Chemistry, and additional studies in English, History, Geography, Mathematics and Drawing. In these early years, students spent only six weeks, soon raised to seven, actually in schools, so that the course concentrated very heavily on general education, with professional educational studies and practice of the skills of teaching playing a very minor part.

The College had two advantages over other training colleges. First of all, as a University institution, it had a much greater freedom to devise its own syllabuses and conduct its own examinations and, very shortly after the First World War, it took advantage of new Board of Education regulations and revised its certificate syllabus in such a way as to enable students to concentrate more on educational matters, both theoretical and practical, and less on specialized subjects or curriculum studies.

Secondly, the College was permitted by the University to teach for University degrees. In 1907, it was given leave to teach for the University's internal Pass Degree in the Arts subjects and, from 1925, for external Pass Degrees in Science. These degree courses had to be taught by 'recognised teachers' of the University. These privileges were a great advantage to the College. Until at least the 1930s, most of the other training colleges had no connection at all with the world of higher education generally, and no incentives to raise their often sadly low academic standards. At Goldsmiths', degree work acted as a powerful academic stimulus for staff and students alike, and helped to prevent the College from becoming as isolated and inbred as many of the other training colleges undoubtedly were.

True, degree students were always in a minority. In 1913 only 3 actually graduated, but the numbers rose steadily after the war to about 50 and by 1938, 60 out of a total of 464 were studying for degrees.

Between the wars, the College expanded its training functions in a number of ways. Refresher courses – what would now be called 'in-service courses' – for teachers were mounted in a number of areas: for the post-war 'continuation' schools, for the teachers of backward children, for teachers in remote rural areas and for missionaries on furlough. From 1922 onwards the College taught for the University Postgraduate Certificate in Education, and from the 1930s for an Art Teacher's Certificate course. Recognising also that, as had not been the case in its early years, many of its students would teach in secondary schools, the College began to run third-year specialist courses in a wide range of subjects, an academic provision which existed hardly anywhere else in the country. It also ran its own Nursery School; and individual members of staff did highly original work on the use of film and radio in schools.

60 Loring Hall in 1938. It was used as a men's hostel from 1938 to 1984. The house was then sold, but the grounds were retained as the College sports ground.

Warden Loring, though a man of authoritarian and unsociable temperament, had very clear ideas about what he wanted the new College to achieve, and very high academic and professional standards. He also had the knack of making good appointments. In theory, in the early years, academic appointments were made by a small committee of the Delegacy, which he was invited to attend. In practice it seems clear that his was the decisive voice. Some of those he appointed moved on to higher things: John Dover Wilson, the eminent Shakespearean scholar, to Chairs at King's College, London, and Edinburgh University, D. L. Savory to the Chair of French at Belfast and ultimately to the House of Commons, J. F. Unstead to the Chair of Geography at Birkbeck College. Men and women appointed to the staff in later years also moved easily upwards in their profession to the principalships of other training colleges; to His Majesty's Inspectorate; and to University Chairs. But it was also a considerable source of strength to the College that many of those appointed by Loring and his successor were to spend most of their working lives in it.

On the outbreak of war in 1914, Loring, a keen amateur soldier who had served with distinction in the Boer War, rejoined his regiment and died of wounds off Gallipoli in 1915. More than 100 former members of the College were also to perish during the war. Thomas Raymont served as Acting

61

62

61 An interior view of Loring Hall.

62 The College Coat of Arms.

Warden until 1919 and then as Warden until he retired two years early in 1927. He was a very different sort of person, by all accounts a quiet and gentle man, far more interested in his teaching than in the financial and administrative problems which successive Wardens had to confront. Late in life, he wrote that he could not say that the years he spent at Goldsmiths' had been pleasant ones. 'It was a happy release for me when I walked out of the place for the last time.'

The third Warden was Arthur Edis Dean. A graduate of Durham University, he had been Professor of Education at University College, Exeter, and, at the time of his appointment to Goldsmiths', was Inspector of Education for Kent County Council. He was an able, energetic and serious-minded man, not without certain useful histrionic qualities. He was not exactly an intellectual, nor anything of a visionary; he saw his job as running the College as effectively and purposefully as possible, more or less along the lines Loring had laid down. Unlike Raymont, he was entirely undaunted by financial problems, and his greatest contribution was probably his success in getting the College rebuilt after the war; tenaciously and endlessly bullying, cajoling, lobbying ministers and officials for the necessary building permits and adequate supplies of building materials and labour. He fully deserved the tribute paid to him on the plaque outside the College gates. He was not, it seems, deeply involved in the operations of the School of Art and the Evening Department, and his grip may have somewhat loosened in his last years, possibly as a result of his membership of a great number of public bodies. He was made a CBE in 1944 and died as a result of a road accident in 1961. He is remembered with deep respect and affection by former students.

In his earlier years, the College – more specifically the Training Department – ran into trouble on two fronts. The national financial crisis of 1931 led to a sharp reduction in the number of students, a sharp increase in fees and a compulsory reduction in staff salaries. Potentially more damaging in the long term was the report of His Majesty's Inspectors, who made their first full visitation of the College in 1937. On academic matters, their report was generally laudatory, but they were sceptical about the value of the degree courses – 'concurrent degree courses did not sit easily with professional training' – and they had sharp criticisms of many of the College facilities: cramped and out-dated accommodation, inadequate sanitary and athletic facilities, poor-quality halls of residence. Apart from the acquisition in 1938 of a new sports ground, little could be done to meet these criticisms before the war and, on this occasion, the University supported the College in its determination to maintain its degree work. But dangers ahead had been clearly signalled.

63 Frederick Marriot, Rue
Gubernatis, Nice.
Etching, 27 x 22 cms.

7 The School of Art: Earlier Decades

64 Paul Drury, self-portrait. Etching, 11 x 7 cms. Drury was a student at Goldsmiths', taught there for many years and was Principal of the School of Art 1967-9.

In 1904, the Goldsmiths' Company had agreed to finance the School of Art, and some of the other activities of its Institute, for one more year, while arrangements for their transfer to the financial control of the LCC were finalised. There was considerable discussion as to what the School of Art should actually do. The Technical Instruction Act of 1889 and the Education Act of 1902 had enabled local authorities to provide Schools of Art, Craft and Design. By 1905 the LCC was maintaining eleven such institutions. Broadly, they gave instruction to three sorts of students: craftsmen or workmen seeking further skills, general students, and practising teachers. The LCC was anxious that the Goldsmiths' School of Art should not compete with its other schools and, at a meeting held in December 1906 between representatives of the Delegacy and the LCC, 'it was agreed that it would be desirable for the Goldsmiths' School of Art to be developed in the direction of higher education in Art including Painting ... Modelling ..., and Design and that any crafts undertaken should be ancillary to the last named and should not be conducted on trade lines'. The meeting also took account, it was reported, 'of the well known preference of workmen for institutions not connected (like the College) with the education of a somewhat higher class'.

In 1912 the Delegacy made a further submission to the Haldane Commission which included a report on the School of Art.

The School of Art provides advanced instruction (the more elementary work having been abandoned in 1904) in Drawing, Painting, Modelling, Design, Book Illustration, Etching, Lithography and Enamelling. There is also a special class in the Methods of Art Teaching. The proportion of 'craft work' to the Painting, Modelling, Design etc. is comparatively small and there are no 'trade' classes.

The report went on to claim that, after a difficult period between 1904 and 1906, the School had 'completely recovered its former position'.

The Delegacy may have been exaggerating the distinction of the School. Certainly, most of the 'trade' classes maintained by the old Institute had gone, and indeed, for many years, it was to be a singular characteristic of the School that very few of its students took any examinations at all or received any nationally

65 William Larkins, A Studio at
Goldsmiths.
21 x 28 cms.

recognised qualifications at the end of their courses. As late as 1958, apart from the 32 students on the Art Teacher's Certificate course, only 34 others took the National Design Diploma examinations, out of a total of 444. Some classes were run for school teachers in art and design, but it was not until the establishment of the Art Teacher's Certificate course in the 1930s that the School made any formal contribution to the training of art teachers in schools. One or two accomplished artists, Harold Speed, a well-known portrait painter, and E. J. Sullivan, a noted book illustrator, were employed as visiting teachers for many years. The Headmaster, Francis Marriott, was a lively figure and a close friend of Arnold Bennett. But he and his successor as Headmaster, W. Amor Fenn (1925-9), had worked at New Cross from 1891. It seems clear that the work of the School under their direction did not change much in its early years as part of Goldsmiths'. Marriott and Amor Fenn were both engravers, and students seem to have been encouraged to specialise in that area of work. The School does not seem to have moved very far in the direction of 'higher education in art'. Graham Sutherland, who entered it as a student in 1921, did not have a high opinion of its quality. In an article written for the catalogue of an exhibition of Clive Gardiner's works held in 1963, he wrote:

While the teaching at the School was probably sound and was certainly practical, it was totally out of touch with the great European movements, then in full flower and moving to a climax. If Old Masters' names were heard I do not remember much serious attempt being made to implant any real understanding of the significance of their work. Still less were we really taught to apply their example to our own work. I do

66 E. Bouverie Hoyton,
Cloutsham. Print, 13 x 15 cms.

67 Robin Tanner, Alington in
Wiltshire.Print, 17 x 22 cms.

66

67

not remember hearing a word about the Impressionists and on the
subject of the Modern Movement there was profound silence.

The development of the School into something altogether
more distinguished was very largely due to Clive Gardiner, a
visiting teacher from 1918, and Headmaster from 1929 until
1958. (His post was upgraded towards the end of his tenure into
a Principalship). He himself was an artist of note, perhaps best

68 Graham Sutherland OM, Hangar Hill. Numbered etching, 14 x 13 cms.

69 Paul Drury, Portrait of his Father in a soft hat, 1935. (Alfred Drury was an eminent sculptor who had himself taught both at the Institute and at the College). Etching, 9 x 10 cms.

70 Paul Drury, Portrait of Carel Weight 1939. Etching, 18 x 12 cms.

71 Graham Sutherland OM, a still life 1948. Pencil, chalks, inks and watercolours, signed in pencil, 50 x 60 cms.

72 Sam Rabin, Boxer entering the ring. Print, 46 x 56 cms.

68

69

70

71

72

73 Adrian Ryan, still life 1949.
Oil on canvas, 38 x 31 cms.

known for the murals he painted for the Wembley Exhibition of 1924 and his posters for London Transport. He was also an excellent and devoted teacher. After Gardiner's death Sutherland told the Warden: 'Everything worthwhile I learnt, I learnt from him'.

Personally unassertive and by no means an enthusiastic administrator – though he did serve as Acting Warden of the College for a term in 1953 – he was a man of wide sympathy and cultivation. Sutherland said that it was from him that one heard for the first time such names as Cézanne and Matisse. In a quiet way, he was also a man of considerable intellectual and social self-confidence, qualities he perhaps derived from his father, A. G. Gardiner, a famous Liberal journalist and editor of the *Daily News*. The style and verve which characterised the School's activities in his time owed much to him. He never attempted to impose his own views on his colleagues and pupils, though his own unreadiness, displayed in his own work, to recognise any important distinction between fine art and commercial art and design was reflected in much of their work too. Certainly, many artists of great distinction worked in the School in his time, as students or teachers, sometimes as both: Rowland Hilder and Sutherland in the 1920s; later Milner Gray, the industrial designer, and Denton Welch, the writer, cruelly injured in a road accident at the end of his second year as a student; Sam Rabin, Carel Weight, Bridget Riley, now an honorary fellow of the College, Mary Quant, the fashion designer; even Tom Keating, the notoriously successful picture faker.

In the 1920s and early 1930s there emerged at Goldsmiths'

74 Clive Gardiner, self-portrait. In oils.

a group of etchers who became known nationally as the 'Goldsmiths' School'. The chief influence on them was the nineteenth-century etcher, Samuel Palmer, and for a time at least the work of this group had a deliberately archaic and pastoral flavour to it, a vision of an idyllic and timeless rural England. Some of them had a good deal in common with Eric Gill and his communities and one or two of them became Roman Catholics. Gardiner himself was involved with their work, as was Sutherland, but otherwise its best known members were Paul Drury, a future Principal, Robin Tanner, William Larkins, also the designer of the wrapping for Black Magic chocolate boxes, and Edward Bouverie-Hoyton.

There was one other important development in Gardiner's time. In 1938, the Board of Education recognised the Art Teacher's Certificate course as one of the sixteen nationally recognised courses undertaking special professional training for qualified students from art schools. It had started a few years earlier as a course for post-diploma students at the Royal College of Art. Reviving after the war, and still happily flourishing, it has been one of the most successful and popular of such courses in the country. It had also, for many years, a peculiar constitutional position within the College. Being regarded as 'academic' in a way that the rest of the School of Art was not, it was fitted up with its own little Academic Board and its own committee structure. Much later, it was reconstructed as a department in the School of Art and, more recently, transferred to the School, later the Faculty, of Education.

75 A photography class before
the First World War.

8 The Decline of Evening Work

As has been shown, things went pretty well for the Training Department and the School of Art between 1905 and 1939. The same was not true of the other activities of the College. Most of the courses run by the Goldsmiths' Institute came to an abrupt end in 1905, though a few mysteriously survived for a brief period: Madam Herring's swimming class for instance, and Miss Robinson's cookery class. But the Science Department which, *inter alia*, taught for matriculation examinations and Pass Degrees of the University, the Engineering Department, which actually taught for Honours Degrees, and the Building Department, were extremely vulnerable. The University acknowledged no financial responsibility for them, and their funding by the LCC depended on the results of difficult and sometimes disappointing annual negotiations. With the terminating of the Goldsmiths' Company's grant in 1912 the writing was on the wall and, by 1915, all degree work outside the Training Department had come to an end.

The students in the Science Department did not go down without a fight, and the proposal finally to close it produced a remarkable reply from them. Some of the opinions expressed in it would be rehearsed many times in future years, but some were more unusual. It was argued that, if evening University Science courses were necessary, which the students thought they were, centralisation could only be effected at New Cross, which was the one and only spot in south-east London which was cheaply and directly accessible from every other. 'It is', they also maintained, 'most highly desirable for both sexes that evening schools should be as far distant as possible from the great centres of gaiety and pleasure.' The students gave notice that they were going to appeal to the LCC.

We shall ask the Council to assist us with that same lavish hand that fosters the education of the feeble-minded, the physically defective and all illiterate aliens. We shall point out that we, at least, do not need promises of social diversions to lure us away from the kinematograph theatres. Our appeal will be justified by earnest work. We are sure, at least, of the sympathies of the local Borough Councils. We further ask the Delegacy to secure the promise of some great public man, that he will head a public appeal for funds should it ultimately be necessary.

From 1915 onwards, the regular activities of the College

76 A plumbing class in the 1920s.

outside the Training Department and the School of Art were concentrated in an Engineering and Building Department, still attracting anything up to 1,000 students annually, but working to a lower academic level than before the war. Its future was always uncertain; as early as 1906 the LCC had declared its intention of creating a new technical college of its own, to which Goldsmiths' departments would be moved. In fact, this plan did not come to anything until 1931, when the South-East London Technical Institute was opened. But, for a brief period after 1918, the Delegacy flirted with a new policy which, had it come to anything, might have fundamentally changed the future development of the College. Daunted by the inability of the University to make capital grants, it approached the LCC with a proposal which, rather surprisingly, also had the endorsement of the University. It suggested that the LCC should abandon its plan for establishing a new technical college of its own, but instead should continue to house, and greatly to extend, such activities on the Goldsmiths' College site. The Delegacy suggested that the College should, in future, provide technical instruction both for junior and more senior students during the day and also in the evening.

The LCC replied enthusiastically, and more or less agreed to provide funds for building and equipment for the new institution. They envisaged an Engineering and Building Department to provide senior evening classes, a junior whole-time day Technical School of Engineering for 200 children and part-time junior day technical classes for the engineering trades. They agreed to maintain the Art Department but insisted that the College should also establish a department for domestic and social science, to provide day and evening classes for women and girls.

This was very much more than the University had bargained for and they quickly withdrew their offer. The Academic Council formally visited the College in November 1919 and came to the conclusion that the main business of the College should continue to be the training of teachers and that a University Institution could not appropriately undertake to provide for the education of boys and girls. As the College's Annual Report for the year 1919-20 recorded: 'The idea of establishing a College of junior day classes had given rise to grave misgiving, because such classes would fall outside the proper province of the University'. And so the matter rested until 1931.

In that year, as a result of prolonged discussions within the College and the LCC, the Peckham and Lewisham Literary Institutes were merged on the College site, which re-opened as the College's Evening Institute, re-christened a few years later as the Evening Department of Adult Education. The LCC undertook to fund it for five years in the first instance. The first Head of the Department worked there for only part of his time; the second remained in post for only two years. As will be shown, the great expansion in this area of College work did not really begin until Ian Gulland, the third Head, returned from the Royal Air Force in November 1945, and so it will be tidier to deal with his remarkable work in a later chapter.

77 War Damage December
1940. The Library.

9 The Second World War

78 An Art and Craft Exhibition held at Nottingham, June 1941.

In the spring of 1939 provisional plans were made for the College to move, in the event of war, to University College, Nottingham, as it then was. And so the autumn term of that year began in Nottingham with the Training Department providing for about 250 women students and 150 men. These numbers were larger than had been expected as the call-up proceeded in a more deliberate way than had perhaps been anticipated. Back in New Cross, the Art School maintained itself in being, as it was to do on a small scale throughout the war. But evening classes were suspended, as Deptford Borough Council had taken over the greater part of the main building for use as an Air Raid Precaution centre, a first aid and casualty clearing station and a canteen open twenty-four hours a day. A unit of the Auxiliary Air Force was also located on the main site and temporary buildings to accommodate it were erected on the back field.

79 A singular watercolour by
M. McCullick entitled Barrage
Balloon backfield, Goldsmiths'
College 1942. 28 x 38 cms.

80 Hugh Stewart Hall in the
1930s. This large hall of
residence was made available by
University College, Nottingham
to Goldsmiths' College for the
whole of the war, and for some
time beyond.

81 H. A. S. Wortley, Principal
of University College,
Nottingham 1935-47. He was a
generous host to Goldsmiths'
College.

82 Professor Victor Murray,
Warden Dean, Canon Hawkins
and Principal Wortley, after a
University Service at St Mary's,
Nottingham, 15 October 1944.

79

By early April 1940, the Delegacy was seriously considering
the return of the Training Department to New Cross: no doubt
the long months of the phoney war made them doubtful of the
need for a prolonged evacuation. Angered by the delay in
reaching a legal agreement with the Deptford Borough Council,
they took the view that 'failing the completion of a satisfactory
agreement, it would be necessary to give the Council three
months' notice to vacate the College buildings'. The same
meeting, probably wisely, took the view that it might not be so
easy to take legal action to evict the Royal Air Force and its
barrage-balloons.

Such ideas had, of course, to be abandoned when 'real war'
broke out in the summer of 1940. True, the School of Art
continued to function – the Delegacy was much put out in
1942 when the Minister of Food appointed Clive Gardiner as
part-time artistic adviser to the Ministry of Food without
consulting the College – and evening classes were resumed on
a modest scale in April 1941. But the prospects of the Training
Department's returning from Nottingham disappeared when
the Luftwaffe began its major bombing campaign in September
1940. From then until May 1941, and again in 1943 and 1944,
south-east London was under almost continuous aerial attack.
Indeed, the worst single incident in the flying bomb and V2
rocket campaign occurred on 25 November 1944 when Woolworths in the New Cross Road (opposite Deptford Town Hall)
took a direct hit, with a resulting loss of 168 lives. The College
buildings had suffered only minor damage during the first year
of the war but on 29 December 1940 – the night on which the
Guildhall was demolished – incendiary bombs set off a fire
which destroyed the roof, the top floor of three sides of the
building, including the library, most of the staff rooms, cloak-

80

81

82

rooms and common rooms and the Chemistry, Biology and Geography classrooms. The School of Art, the Great Hall and some other buildings, including the kitchens, survived, but the greater part of the College had become little more than a ruin. Further serious damage was done in 1944, and in May 1945 the swimming baths were totally destroyed.

The College, and especially Warden Dean, remained determined to return to New Cross as soon as possible, but even after the war had ended there were huge problems about obtaining building permits and licences, and the necessary labour and materials. Moreover, 'Londoners' Meals Service' which took over the kitchens from the Deptford Borough Council after the 1940 bombing, were extremely reluctant to depart, and their presence in the College until late 1945 seems seriously to have hampered repair operations. There were

83

83 The destruction of
Woolworths in the New Cross
Road, 25 November 1944.

84 Major-General Sir Frederick
Maurice, fifth Chairman of the
Delegacy 1931-44, Principal of
the East London College, later
Queen Mary College 1933-44.
Portrait by Henry Lamb.

85 The first royal visit to
Goldsmiths' College.

86 The plaque outside the
College, commemorating
Warden Dean's success in
getting the College restored
after the war.

87 Post-war high rise building
in Deptford.

84

those, indeed, who never expected to see the College re-
established in New Cross at all. In June 1943, the Mayor of
Deptford summoned a conference at the Town Hall to consider
the possibilities of developing a community centre, particularly for young people, and asked whether there was any

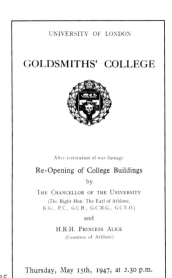

87

chance of the Borough's acquiring the College buildings for that purpose. In the following January, the Town Clerk of Deptford served a Requisition Order on the College to acquire the Lecture Hall and some other rooms to provide for an extension to the part-time nursery being conducted by the Borough Council. On this occasion, however, the Board of Education supported the Warden in his opposition to this plan; mainly, it appears, on the technical ground that the Ministry of Health, in sanctioning the proposal, had failed to observe the Cabinet instruction 'that no requisition of an educational building can be approved without prior consultation with the Board of Education'. But these incidents show how little confidence was felt locally in the future of Goldsmiths' College at New Cross. And, indeed, it was not until the autumn term of 1946 that the full range of College activities was resumed on the New Cross site. First-year students had returned to a still largely ruinous and chaotic building for the summer term of that year, but a year later most of the war-time damage had been repaired and, on 15 May 1947, 250 dignitaries from the University, the Ministry of Education, the Goldsmiths' Company, the LCC and other local authorities were entertained to tea in the newly restored library, to celebrate the return. The Warden spoke at some length and the Chancellor of the University, the Earl of Athlone, spoke in warm terms of the College and of its future role, though perhaps it was more true than tactful for him to begin his oration by reminding his audience 'that the tide of University traffic in this great City of London flows, in the main, on the north side of the Thames' and that the University was therefore but seldom able to make formal visitations to its outposts, so that gatherings of the kind held that day had not been frequent at New Cross.

88 *Trial by Jury* 1908.

10 College Life: The First Few Decades

The College Hymn

In the vapour of the furnace he must wrestle with his work,
Where amid the unwrought metal countless forms of beauty lurk;
To shape them and adorn them is the task he may not shirk:
    The smith is working on.

Sitting daily by his anvil he pursues his ceaseless quest,
His joy is in his craftsmanship, the mystery's touch impressed;
But still the elusive masterpiece will never let him rest:
    The smith is working on.

The beating of the hammer in his ear for ever cries,
The heavenly patterned vessel hangs before his dreaming eyes;
His heart is set on perfecting his golden enterprise:
    The smith is working on.

We work in richer metal, by a greater anvil stand
As we seek to fashion children for a finer, nobler land;
Till the mystic touch approves them from the Master Craftsman's hand
    The 'Smiths are working on.

This hymn was written by Miss Caroline Graveson, Women's Vice-Principal from 1905 to 1934. Music was specially composed for it by a former student, but it was more commonly sung to the tune of 'John Brown's Body'.

A College Song

'SMITHS ARE WE!

This is the song we love to sing whenever the mood comes o'er us,
Making the grand old college ring with its rollicking roaring chorus,
    its rollicking roaring chorus.

'Smiths are we, 'Smiths are we, Proud of our College as proud can be,
One and all we'll stand or fall, Fall or stand together!
'Smiths are we, 'Smiths are we, Jolly good fellows as you may see!
No matter the weather we'll stand together for 'Smiths are we!
    'Smiths are we!

This is the song with which full oft
Valorous foes are daunted,
When from the field it ascends aloft
And the pride of the 'Smiths is vaunted.
    Chorus

Wherever we wander near or far,
Leaving the Col. behind us,

89 Warden Loring commanded the College Cadet Corps which was affiliated to a territorial battalion of the Royal West Kent Regiment, the Queen's Own.

What we have been, and what still are
The lilt of it will remind us.
        Chorus

    This is the song we love to raise
At any and every season,
Who sings not this best of a thousand lays
Most surely is guilty of treason.
        Chorus

This was written by A. J. A. Wilson (1906-1908), and set to music by a contemporary, Rowland J. Rowlands.

These two sets of verses illustrate well two salient characteristics of the College in its earlier years. Loring and his colleagues had been resolved to develop among staff and students alike a deep sense of moral and civic purpose and strong loyalties to the College as an institution, and they succeeded to a remarkable extent. To some degree, these objects were to be achieved by the adoption of rules and conventions which might now seem unduly rigorous in a particularly old-fashioned boarding school. All students and staff attended Morning Assembly at which hymns were sung and uplifting addresses or readings given. It is said that Warden Dean particularly favoured the Book of Job and the sermons of John Donne. All students had to attend the mid-day meal, presided over by the Warden and his senior colleagues, begowned at the High Table; lecturers in the School of Art had a separate less high table of their own. Segregation of the sexes was maintained as strictly as possible. Separate lectures – all tuition in the early days was done by means of the formal lecture – were

90 Water polo 1906-7.

91 Tennis during the First World War.

92 The College hockey XI during the 1933-34 session, with Mr R. A. Raven, Men's Vice-Principal 1930-39.

90

91

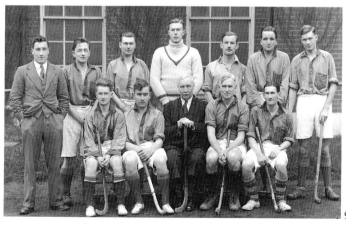

92

93 *The Yeoman of the Guard* 1941. A joint production by students of University College, Nottingham, the Institute of Education and Goldsmiths' College.

94 A Victorian Ball, December 1949 with the Warden and Mrs Dean in the forefront.

93

94

given for men and women students. The building itself was in effect divided into two halves, the north side being reserved for men and the south side for women, and there were strict rules against any crossing of the lines of demarcation. At Morning Assembly, and again in the Refectory, men and women students were forbidden to sit next to each other. Not until 1929 was a single Students' Union established. Indeed, until a Men's Union and a Women's Union were set up in 1924, the responsibility for organising student activities lay with two Senior Prefects appointed by the Warden.

Life in the student hostels was also rigorously controlled. As late as 1930, students could only be absent from meals with special permission and, in any event, were expected to have returned by 9 pm in the summer and by 8 pm in the other terms. Silence had to be observed at stated times and all lights to be put out by 10.30 at the latest. On one night only was late theatre leave given, and there were complicated rules about such things as the making and changing of beds, the airing of rooms, laundry and so forth. Most students slept in dormitories and as late as the mid-1950s there were great doubts as to whether they should have keys to their own living quarters. The hostels were seen as serving a purpose more elevated than simply providing students with somewhere to live in suitably regulated conditions. The Heads of the Hostels or Halls had a key role in fostering the moral, and to some extent the intellectual qualities of the students. As late as the mid-1950s, Warden Price was to be unhappy about a new plan to centralise the financial and administrative arrangements governing the Halls, on the grounds that it might undermine the moral authority of the Heads.

Right from the beginning, it was the College's plan to house all students in the Training Department in College hostels. And, indeed, this remained the policy until well into the 1960s. It was particularly important for the College to try to implement it in the early years because of a Board of Education regulation that female students in Day Training Colleges must either be housed in College hostels or live at home. But there were great difficulties. Public grants to help with the acquisition and conversion of suitable properties could only be made to local authorities. And the College, especially in the early years, had no funds of its own for these purposes.

The first three hostels, all opened in 1907, were provided by the Kent and Surrey County Councils and by the National Society. (The National Society's hostel, St Michael's, was finally given up in 1939, and it should be recorded that former students who had lived there made very generous donations to the College Library Appeal of 1986). Middlesex County Council provided a hostel in 1911, the College rented a large property known as 'The Grove' in Blackheath and, in 1912, the Goldsmiths' Company bought two properties for use as hostels, one in Blackheath and one (Pentland House) in Old Road, Lee.

Pentland House had an interesting past. From the late seventeenth century it had been owned by a naval family of Wiltshire origins called Smith. In the nineteenth century it had passed into the ownership of the Baring family. Educational activities were carried on there during the Napoleonic wars, when a French refugee, a M. Grimaldi, had conducted a 'School of Deportment for Young Ladies of Fashion', under the rather surprising patronage of Princess, later Queen, Caroline of Brunswick, the Prince Regent's unruly wife.

The other hostel provided by the Goldsmiths' Company, in

95 A production by speech and drama students of *Macbeth* 1952.

Westcombe Park Road, Blackheath, was the first men's hostel. Shortly after the First World War, with the further help of Kent County Council, the College was able to open two more hostels, and by 1921, 341 of the women students in the Training Department were housed in College residences, out of a total of 368; and 76 male students out of a total of 173. No further changes were made before 1939 except that, as has been said, the National Society gave up St Michael's hostel in 1939 and, more importantly, at the same time, the College acquired a handsome eighteenth-century house some ten miles away, at North Cray, for use as a men's hostel. In the early nineteenth century it had belonged to Lord Castlereagh and was, in fact, the scene of his suicide. The main reason for this purchase had been that the house – renamed Loring Hall in memory of the first Warden – had an agreeable, small park attached to it, which is still used as the College's main sports ground.

One of the smaller halls of residence was entirely demolished by bombing in 1940, but otherwise the position remained the same until the great building spree of the early 1960s.

Loring and his colleagues intended right from the start to foster the growth of what might be called a 'College Spirit'. Many of the students in the early years had little in the way of secondary education and had everything to learn about intel-

96 Programme of the College
Open Day held on 9 June 1956.

PROGRAMME OF EVENTS

2 - 3	RECEPTION OF VISITORS ...	...	GREAT HALL
2.30 - 3.5	a. THE DRAMATIC SOCIETY will present "Two Gentlemen of Soho" *By A. P. Herbert* Produced by Mr. M. P. Burger		... SMALL HALL
	b. FILM SHOW: ... ... The art of Graham Sutherland		... ROOM 99
2.30 - 3.15	ROUNDERS Final of Inter-Hostel Tournament		LOWER FIELD
3.0 - 4.0	BASKETBALL: Exhibition Match Goldsmiths' v. Midfield Old Boys (Kent County Junior Champions)		
3.15 - 5.0	TEA		... REFECTORY
3.30 - 4.5	a. THE DRAMATIC SOCIETY will present "The Stepmother" *By Arnold Bennett* Produced by Mr. M. Clarke ...		.. SMALL HALL
	b. FILM SHOW: ... .. The art of Graham Sutherland		... ROOM 99
4.30 - 5.5	THE DRAMATIC SOCIETY will present ... "Two Gentlemen of Soho" *By A. P. Herbert* Produced by Mr. M. P. Burger		... SMALL HALL
4.45 - 5.5	WOMEN'S VAULTING DISPLAY	..	GREAT HALL
5.5 - 5.25	MEN'S AGILITY AND VAULTING DISPLAY		GREAT HALL
5.25 - 5.45	MODERN EDUCATIONAL DANCE		... GREAT HALL
6.0 - 6.15	ADDRESS BY THE WARDEN ...		.. GREAT HALL
6.15 - 7.0	CONCERT		GREAT HALL

Seating accommodation in the Small Hall is limited. Doors will be
open 15 minutes before each of the Dramatic Performances.

lectual and cultural matters not touched on in their school
classrooms. Some of them for example had hardly read a word
of English literature. So he and his colleagues took the lead in
developing all kinds of non-academic corporate activities, a
Literary and Debating Society, Musical and Dramatic Societies,
Athletic Clubs and the like. He himself raised and commanded
an Officers Training Corps. No doubt this corporate College
spirit sometimes manifested itself in a sort of rugger club

rowdiness. But the testimony of early generations of students does show that these efforts were remarkably successful. The way in which the Old Students' Association flourished during its first six decades also shows how warmly its members felt about the College.

It was founded in 1907, as soon as the first generation of students – 'the aborigines' – had completed their course. It flourished until the First World War, then fell into something of a decline but recovered strongly in Warden Dean's time. It held an Annual Reunion sometimes attended by as many as 1,000 members, organised an Educational Conference in March each year, at which the staff of the College, members of the Association (these being, of course, mainly teachers) and other members of the profession deliberated and were lectured to on subjects of current professional interest. Until well into the 1950s surviving aborigines held a luncheon in College and, during the same years, there was also held a Jubilee Luncheon each year attended by staff and students who had entered the College fifty years before – a practice which still continues. An annual journal and newsletter was published and the Association, apart from its formal meetings, clearly maintained quite a lively social life.

This was true of the College also. As has been indicated, life was far more formal than it subsequently became. Besides the daily rituals of the Morning Assembly and the Mid-day Meal, there was, for instance, an annual Foundation Day Oration, at which students and their parents, and the staff in full academicals, heard addresses from notable persons, like the then Sir Anthony Blunt, who in 1966, asked them 'Is Art History Bunk?' There was a formal Ball held each year in the Great Hall and similar more modest but equally formal occasions in the hostels, which still continue. There was a College Sports Day, attended by all staff and students, held after the Second World War at Loring Hall, where tea was served on the terraces and proceedings concluded with a buffet supper and dance. At Christmas, staff and students took it in turns to wait on each other at luncheon, and, in the summer, the School of Art provided a whole series of entertainments, Mediaeval Pageants, Toy Theatres, elaborate Tea Parties and an ambitious Summer Ball. So life was festive as well as formal and, it seems, rather jolly.

11 Post-War Restoration

97 Sir Stanley Marchant,
the sixth Chairman of the
Delegacy 1944-49, and
Principal of the Royal Academy
of Music 1936-49.

98 Aubrey Joseph Price,
Warden of the College 1950-53,
portrait in oils by Clive
Gardiner.

In retrospect it can be seen that these were relatively quiet years, during which the College carried on in very much the same way as in the 1920s and 1930s. Only in the late 1950s did clear signs of impending upheaval appear. So it will be convenient to review, briefly, the main areas of College activity in those last fifteen or so years of the old order.

Most remarkable were the developments that took place in the Evening Department. It made a tolerably good start in 1931, attracting in the last year before the war about 1400 students. University extension classes were revived, though some lecturers were not impressed by the quality of the students or the Department's administrative arrangements. The war had pretty well put an end to its activities and it was Ian Gulland who really got it going after he returned from the war in November 1945. He had been appointed in 1938, having been previously a tutor in the East Midlands branch of the Workers' Educational Association and then a lecturer in the Department of Extra-Mural Studies at University College, Nottingham. He was extremely efficient and hardworking and ran his Department pretty well single-handed. He was a learned man with catholic taste and a profound belief in the moral, democratic and entertainment values of adult education. He was not given to deep pronouncements on the subject; he would, no doubt, have understood, but would almost certainly not have used, the phrase 'seamless robe' to describe the impossibility of distinguishing between various sorts of educational activities. As a friend and colleague said of him, so far as the boundaries of adult education were concerned, he remained a pragmatist. Characteristically, he made it his business to involve students in deciding what courses the Department should mount, and how and when they should be run. He was, in a mild way, something of an eccentric.

By 1950, the number of enrolled students had risen to about 3300. Something of the flavour of the Evening Department's activities can be caught from its prospectus for 1956, printed on page 86 below.

By that session, evening classes were being given in a wide range of subjects. There were 15 classes on Philosophy, Psychology, Religious Studies; 8 on English Literature and Written

99 The academic staff of the College in 1954.

English; 14 on Speech Training, Play Reading, Stage Craft and Puppets; there were 5 classes on English for Foreigners, 5 on Classical Languages and no fewer than 36 on Modern European Languages. There were 11 classes on History, Archaeology, Geography and Field Studies and 11 on Science; also 6 on the Arts. There was also an ambitious musical programme dealing with appreciation and theory, piano instruction, instrumental instruction and instruction in solo and choral singing. There was quite a programme of physical education, including sword and Morris dancing and advanced fencing. Finally, there was a big programme in educational teaching, the classes being principally intended for teachers in schools. There was also an ambitious programme of University Extension courses, arranged with the co-operation of the Department of Extra-Mural Studies in London University. These courses dealt with subjects very similar to those of the ordinary evening classes; in some cases, they could lead to an examination for a University Diploma. Their distinguishing characteristic was that they required more active study from the students following them and some of them extended over periods as long as three years.

The Department was extremely active in advertising its wares, and the Evening Students' Association took a large part in this activity. It was they who organised an annual Open Day – or Rally, as it was called – at which all kinds of activities were displayed, presumably with a view to attracting clients. On 9 May 1953, for example, no fewer than four concerts were given; lectures on, amongst other things, modern home furnishings, bamboo pipes and music; a philosophical discussion on 'Objective Standards in Morals'; exhibitions of old-time dancing; a variety programme presented by the German and Spanish Societies; and an exhibition of the night sky in

100

101

100 Sir John Lockwood, the eighth Chairman of the Delegacy 1951-58, Master of Birkbeck College and Vice-Chancellor 1955-58.

101 The Chairman of the Delegacy introducing Sir Philip Morris, who delivered the Jubilee Oration on 7 June 1955.

May, presented by the Astronomical Society. After the concert in the Great Hall, which consisted of four works by Handel, one by Elgar and two by Vaughan Williams, there was informal dancing in the Great Hall until 11 pm, arranged by the Ballroom Dancing Club.

Gulland also organised walking tours, visits to historical and archaeological sites, weekend conferences and foreign tours. Good fun, it seems fair to say, could be had by all and there are obviously resemblances between the operations of Gulland's Department and those of the Goldsmiths' Institute half a century earlier.

Some account of the School of Art, up to Clive Gardiner's retirement in 1958, has already been given. But the Training Department remained at the heart of the College, its *raison d'être*. Numbers of students rose to well over 600 and almost all of them were taking the two-year Certificate course, though some of them would follow with a third-year specialised course and more than 100 combined it with an external degree course of the University. In 1957-8, only nineteen students were engaged on the Postgraduate Diploma of Education course. A number of special short courses were being run, but the emphasis of activity remained very much as it had been before the war.

One new element in the Training Department's affairs had been introduced in 1947. A committee chaired by the Vice-Chancellor of Liverpool University had reported in 1944 that it thought it would be a good plan if the Universities were more involved in the training of teachers but, unfortunately, both his committee, and almost everyone else concerned, were sharply divided as to how, and to what extent, this involvement should be brought about. The solution eventually adopted was that

102

103

102 Sir Henry Tizard, Prime
Warden of Goldsmiths'
Company (left) presenting the
Warden of the College, Dr D. R.
Chesterman, with a silver rose
bowl on 7 June 1955, to mark
the College's Jubilee.

103 Ian Gulland, Principal of
the Evening Department 1938-
70, painted by John Mansbridge.

104 Part of the Evening
Department prospectus for
1956.

THE OBJECTS OF THE EVENING DEPARTMENT

The main purpose of the Evening Department is to enable men and
women to widen their knowledge and interests and to enrich and enjoy
their leisure time. This object is achieved primarily through the provision
of non-vocational classes. Obviously, some of the classes shown in this
prospectus, particularly those for teachers, have a practical as well as
a purely cultural value ; but in the main the curriculum aims not at
preparing students for examinations, but at supplying opportunities for
mental and physical activity and for a rational approach to the fundamental moral, social, political and economic issues of our time.

The Evening Department also attempts to fulfil its purpose by offering
facilities for the development of a social and cultural community life,
based on the refectory, the common rooms, the concert hall, library and
theatre ; on the active co-operation of students, through such elected
representative bodies as the Evening Students' Association, and the
Class Representatives' Council ; and on the self-governing students' clubs. 104

the Training Colleges should be grouped together in Institutes
of Education established by local Universities, these Institutes
being subject to the scrutiny of a National Advisory Council
on the training and supply of teachers. So, the College's
Training Department became also a Department of the London
University Institute and members of its staff found that they
had to learn new administrative and academic parts.

Shortly after this, they received a nasty setback. Unexpectedly, as a result of discussions on financial problems, the
University suddenly intimated that Goldsmiths' College
students should no longer read for internal degrees of the
University. The College protested, but, following a formal
visitation headed by the Principal, Dr Douglas Logan, and the
Chairman of the Academic Council, Professor Hale Bellot, the
Senate confirmed the decision in 1950. The grounds were clear
enough. It was 'not convinced that the College gained a great
deal from conducting general degree courses for a comparatively small number of students'. It felt that its library and
laboratory facilities were simply not adequate and that it
would have to divert too many of its resources from what
remained its main purpose, the training of teachers, if it was to
bring them up to scratch. So Dean's wardenship – he finally
retired in 1950 – ended on a rather sour note.

The decision had one curious, and very probably unforeseen,
constitutional effect. As the last generation of students fin-
ished their degree courses the 'recognised teachers' who had
been responsible for their tuition lost that status on the logical
enough grounds that they no longer had any degree students to
teach. How, though, the position of the College as an Institution with Recognised Teachers was to be sustained once it
had ceased to contain any such persons is an interesting
question.

This weakening of the academic links between the College

105 John Mansfield, Chief Accountant 1915-56, painted by Clive Gardiner.

106 Alfred Mansfield, Assistant Accountant and Registrar of the School of Art 1914-58, painted by Clive Gardiner.

and the University had been preceded during and just after the war by another brisk round of discussions on constitutional matters. It all started with the bombing. How was the College to find the money to repair the damage and get going again? (It was not supposed that government compensation grants would be adequate.) A dramatic meeting took place in January 1943 in the College ruins between members of the University Court and the College Delegacy. There was general agreement that the College should be restored, and it was decided to approach the University Grants Committee and try to persuade it to regard the College as an appropriate recipient for its funds. The answer was very firmly in the negative. So, in December 1944, a joint deputation from the University and the College went to the Ministry of Education to discuss the problems of future funding. The Ministry, regarding the University as the providing authority, expected it to produce the capital needed for major building projects, but the University, not being able to apply for UGC funding for such purposes, was only able to help to a very limited extent. Another approach was made to the Ministry in the summer of 1947, but again the results were unsatisfactory as all the Ministry did was to suggest that another approach should be made to the UGC. And, once again, the answer was in the negative. The University itself then became alarmed, fearing that the College might become a serious financial burden on it and, in October 1948, the Court took the view that the position of the College as an institution owned by the University, but financially dependent on the Ministry of Education and the LCC, was becoming increasingly anomalous. It was even agreed to ask Dean to stay on for an extra two years, on the grounds that it would be impossible to advertise for a successor until the constitutional position of the College had been finally clarified.

In fact, the immediate financial problem was solved in 1949 by an agreement between the Treasury and the Ministry of Education, which enabled the Ministry to pay full capital grants to the College for new building and repairs, etc. But the constitutional position of the College had still not been clarified, and was indeed to remain anomalous for almost another forty years.

Aubrey Joseph Price became the fourth Warden of the College in 1950. He had previously been Headmaster of St Peter's School, York, and of Wellington School, Somerset. Between 1947 and 1950 he was Principal of Wymondham Emergency Training College. He remained at Goldsmiths' for only seven terms before moving to an Anglican Training College in Chester and taking Holy Orders. He did not have time to make much mark on the College's affairs. Problems to

107 Mr F. G. Chanter, who worked for the College for 50 years up to 1957, speaking at his retirement dinner.

do with the administration of the College hostels needed a lot of his attention, and it has been suggested that he found senior members of the College staff – well entrenched in powerful positions by Dean's later years – rather a handful. He was rather too much of the Anglican headmaster to accommodate himself readily to the College's very different traditions. It is possible, too, that he would have found his job easier if Dean had not continued to take such a keen and active interest in College affairs. However, his successor, Dr Ross Chesterman, was well established by the time the College celebrated its Jubilee in the summer of 1955.

Since 1904 the Governing Body had been a committee of the Senate of the University, known as the Delegacy. It had been enlarged several times but the general pattern of membership and the terms of reference, decided on in 1904, remained broadly the same. The Chairmen of the Delegacy had generally been senior members of the University, the exceptions being Lord Perry of Walton (1981-84) and Sir Charles Carter (1984-). Sometimes the Vice-Chancellor himself held the chairmanship, sometimes the heads of other great London colleges. In the early years, attendance at Delegacy meetings tended to be sparse; at one stage, Sidney Webb and Sir William Hart Dyke attended only one of eighteen meetings to which they were summoned. The Delegacy did not, until 1963, establish any junior committees, but it seems that a lot of its work was done by direct contact between the Warden of the day and one or two particularly keen delegates: Sir Walter Prideaux for instance, and Professor Graham Wallas, the social scientist, himself Chairman of the Delegacy from 1924 to 1928. Other Chairmen who worked extremely hard in the College's interests were Major-General Sir Frederick Maurice of Queen Mary College, 1931-44, and Dr J. F. Lockwood, Master of Birkbeck and later Vice-Chancellor, 1951-58.

This system gave considerable power to any Warden who cared to exercise it. He was the only member of the College staff in direct contact with the Governing Body – until 1935 as an officer in attendance, thereafter as a full member. Nor were the College's internal arrangements markedly democratic. An Academic Board was not established until 1935, though there had long been a Staff Council and, from 1948, an Advisory Staff/Student Council. All the same, Warden Chesterman could record that when he arrived in the College in 1953, there were very few committees. (A happy fault, of which the College was very soon most earnestly to repent.) A proposal made as late as 1957 that two members of the academic staff of the College, in addition to the Warden, should be added to the Delegacy ran aground because of the objections of the LCC representatives. Dr – later Sir – Isaac Hayward told the Delegacy that he took strong exception to the proposal. 'It was contrary to the policy of the LCC to have any employee, whether lecturer, teacher or in any other capacity, serving on the Governing Bodies of colleges, institutions or schools.' He implied that the Council had made a considerable concession in allowing principals of institutions to be *ex officio* members of Governing Bodies and did not wish to go beyond that.

Up to the mid 1950s or so, educational administration was much less complicated than it later became. Much of the work later done by administrative officers was in the hands of the two Vice-Principals. For over forty years, such administration as was done was the responsibility of the two Mansfield brothers: John, who was Chief Accountant from 1915 to 1956, and Alfred, who was Assistant Accountant and Registrar of the School of Art from 1914 to 1958. Mr F. G. Chanter, Registrar of the Training Department, worked in the College for a full half century but it does not appear that the Mansfields ever regarded him as quite being an equal.

John and Alfred were a remarkable pair. Their responsibilities were chiefly financial or related strictly to the registration of students. They performed these duties in a room at the front of the building, the door of which they kept firmly locked against all those who did not know the secret knock which gained admission. It is said that they wore bowler hats during the solemn ceremony of the daily opening of the College mail. It is also recorded that, on one occasion, Warden Dean forgot the secret knock and, for all his clamours, could not persuade the Mansfields to open the door to him. He retreated, defeated, to his upstairs office and spoke so irately down the speaking tube that he actually blew it off the wall of the two Mansfields' office. During the war, John, disdaining the safety of Nottingham, continued to work in College as the buildings were blown up around him; Alfred was seconded to work for Deptford Borough Council. They returned readily to their former routines after the war and would, it appears, have been more than happy to work on after retirement age.

But they would not have found it easy to deal with the new conditions of the 1960s. A new generation of academic administrators took up their posts from 1957 onwards, notably Mr J. L. Coleman, as Bursar, and Mr W. H. Jones, ultimately to be designated Academic Registrar. Even more important was the arrival of George Cecil Wood as the first Registrar of the College in 1958. He had read Physics at New College, Oxford, and had gone to Gordon College, Khartoum, as Head of the Physics Department. He then moved to administrative matters and left Khartoum when it was reconstituted as an independent University. Wood was to be one of the key figures in College history, but his time has yet to come and this section will end with the College's Jubilee celebrations of 1955.

They began with an Open Day on Saturday, 4 June, attended by 1400 people; there were plays, films, athletic and dance displays; a reception given by the Warden and a concert in the evening. On the following Monday, 150 past and present members of the staff, together with many academic and civic dignitaries, dined in the Goldsmiths' Company's Hall. On Tuesday 7 June, Sir Philip Morris, the Vice-Chancellor of Bristol University, gave the 'Foundation Oration' in the Great Hall on the 'Education of Teachers', and the Prime Warden of the Goldsmiths' Company, Sir Henry Tizard, presented the Warden with a silver rose bowl. There was a Jubilee Concert on the Thursday, an Open Debate on the Friday, and proceedings were concluded with a Jubilee Ball on the Saturday, organised by the Students' Union. All week, exhibitions of the College's work were on display and four performances of the *Oresteia* were given. Nor was the enthusiasm for celebrating the first fifty years exhausted by that crowded week. The November reunion of the Old Students' Association was attended by more than 1000 people, and thirty of the aboriginals, together with five members of the original staff, sat down to luncheon together. Chesterman's observation, at the beginning of Jubilee week, was surely well founded: 'One of the acid tests of a College is the degree of affection and loyalty it is able to inspire in its students. By this test, Goldsmiths' does not fail.'

Part Two

108 The Lockwood building
(1962), built to house
gymnasia and craft studios.

12 Introduction

The last thirty years have been a time of almost continuous change, not to say upheaval, in the whole British educational system. In the 1960s and early 1970s there was growth and development, and a good deal of money about; since then, there have been retrenchment, contraction, and severe financial constraints. Broadly speaking, events at Goldsmiths' followed a similar pattern, with a good many complications and variations thrown in. It would have made for a shapelier and more symmetrical text if it could be claimed that everything that happened did so in accordance with a coherent long-term plan, and that all the decisions taken by the College and other authorities were wise ones. Unfortunately, neither proposition could be sustained. There had to be major and sudden changes of policy and a good deal of 'crisis management'. And with so many balls in the air, it is not surprising that, from time to time, one or two of them were dropped.

13 New Buildings

109 The Whitehead building (1968) was built as a science and administration block.

In 1957 the government made the long expected announcement that, from 1960 onwards, the two-year Certificate of Education course would be extended by a year. This at once made the size of the Training Department a live issue. If the number of students was not to be increased by 50 per cent, the number of teachers the College would produce would actually fall. But, to begin with, the Ministry of Education ruled that the total number of students in training must not rise beyond 750, from a total of 631 in 1957-8. At the same time it warned the College that no further expansion could be anticipated for at least thirty years!

It was a singularly inaccurate prediction. Over the next ten years or so, student numbers in the Training Department rose, at the behest of government, to 1234 in 1964-5, and to almost 2000 in 1969-70. And there was a more or less proportionate increase in academic and administrative staff.

The most lasting and visible effects of these decisions were the new buildings that had to be put up to accommodate the increased numbers. The Department of Education and Science (which replaced the Ministry of Education in 1964) worked to

110 The Warmington Tower (1969) is the College's only high-rise hall of residence. There are fine views from the upper floors.

111 St James's Hall (1962).

112 The Ceramics building (1980).

113 The College Gallery (1975).

110

111

112

113

114

115

114   The author (right) taking the Rt Hon Peter Brooke MP, then Parliamentary Under-Secretary of State at the Department of Education and Science, around the new Refectory on 7 November 1983.

115   Refectory after a major refurbishment carried out in 1983.

less generous scales in providing funds for building projects than the UGC was enabled to do in relation to the Universities, and though not all the new University buildings of the 1960s were things of beauty, or are likely to prove joys for ever, they were generally built to more lavish standards than Goldsmiths' could afford. The College's new buildings were mainly designed by the firm of Enthoven and Mock and were for the most part serviceable enough, but certainly did not have the distinction of the work of Shaw and Blomfield.

Several of them were put up immediately to the north-west of Shaw's main building. The Education building was completed in 1968 – a further floor was added later – together with the Gallery; a new, high-rise hall of residence (the Warmington Tower) went up in 1969 and an extension to the Students' Union in 1975. The old chapel building was converted into a theatre in 1964, and new accommodation was provided for Music, Drama and Geography. The kitchens and the refectory were reorganised more than once.

Two larger new buildings were erected on the south-west and north-west sides of the back field: a Gymnasium and Craft block in 1962, with an extension being added in 1972 (the Lockwood Building), and a Science and Administration block (the Whitehead Building) in 1968. Two other new halls of residence were built; St James's (near the church) in 1963, and Raymont Hall, a mile or so away in Brockley. Pentland House and Surrey House were considerably enlarged and, in 1980, the DES, rather unexpectedly, produced funding for a fine new ceramics building on one of the terraces above the back field. Also, a considerable number of useful houses in the immediate vicinity of the College were acquired, in many cases as a result of ingenious initiatives by the Registrar, George Wood.

116

117

Some major plans foundered, however. Further developments
planned in the area of the Education building and of St James's
Church came to nothing; which was perhaps just as well, as the
sites were later to be used for the new Library and new buildings
for the Laban Centre of Movement and Dance. More serious was
the collapse in 1974 for financial reasons, after many years of
planning and negotiation with the LCC and then the ILEA, of
the project to erect a new School of Art building above the back
field. It would have squared off the College's campus in a neat
way, would have made the subsequent dispersion of important
activities unnecessary and, as will be seen, would have saved

118 An aerial view of the College taken before the building of the new Library.

the School of Art from many years of travelling from one site to another.

Instead, the College had the use for a period of twelve years or so of two substantial buildings at Deptford and Camberwell, as a result of an amalgamation in 1977 with two former Colleges of Education. To the Rachel McMillan building in Deptford went two of the Science Departments and to the St Gabriel's building in Camberwell – renamed the Millard building – went a large part of the School of Art. Considerable sums were expended by the DES on fitting out these buildings for their new purposes. No-one could then foresee that, as a result of further changes in policy, the Millard building would be sold in 1988 and the Deptford building made over to Thames Polytechnic. The building of a new library did in the 1980s, however, make it possible for the whole of the School of Art to be reunited with the rest of the College on the main site in 1988.

14 The Training of Teachers

119 Sir Ross Chesterman, Warden of the College 1953-74, Hon Fellow of the College 1974.
Portrait in oils by Bernard Hailstone, himself a long-serving teacher at the College.

To revert to the affairs of the Training Department. Much had, of course, to be done simply in devising the new three-year Certificate of Education course and in coping with the expansion in staff and student numbers. But new prospects opened up with the publication, in October 1963, of the Robbins Report on Higher Education. In respect of the training of teachers, it recommended an increase of almost 200 per cent in student numbers. It took the view that 750 was the minimum viable student enrolment for training colleges; it applauded, and wished to see widely extended, the practice of colleges offering four-year courses, in which professional training and degree work would be combined; it proposed an entirely new degree course, to be called the Bachelor of Education degree; and it suggested means by which far closer links could be established between the universities and the training colleges.

All this seemed to vindicate policies already adopted by the College. It was large and growing; it already ran four-year concurrent courses; and it had pretty close links with London University. There were, however, to be problems. London University quickly moved to establish a B Ed degree, which students at training colleges in the London area could read for. But as it was a University degree course, the syllabus and regulations were determined by the University, and it took some time to integrate the College's existing courses with the new University degree. Also, it became necessary for College staff engaged in teaching for the new four-year concurrent courses to become 'Recognised Teachers'. Recognition was granted chiefly on the basis of postgraduate qualifications or academic research. So a period of hectic activity set in, in which books and articles were published, Masters' degrees obtained, doctoral theses submitted.

All the same, the 1960s were good years for the Training Department. The proportion, as well as the numbers, of students on the concurrent courses increased sharply. Standards of professional and academic work kept improving. A number of important public projects were undertaken, including the preparation of various reports for the Schools' Council, and notably, the establishment, at the request of the DES in 1965, of what became known as the Curriculum Laboratory. This began

120

121

120 Goldsmiths' College
Play Centre, 1957.

121 The Education building
was put up in two stages
between 1968 and 1975.

as a series of courses for serving teachers, intended to help prepare them for the raising of the school-leaving age to sixteen planned for 1972. It developed into a sort of forum in which ideas about the future development of school curricula were debated, and its activities were chronicled in a publication sponsored by the College called *Ideas*. There was in fact a general sense of purposeful advance.

The Department even got a grand new name. In 1965, the government accepted one of the Robbins Committee's recommendations and decided that, in future, Training Colleges would be known as Colleges of Education. That would have been an inappropriate name for Goldsmiths', which also, of course, had its School of Art and its Evening Department. So, after much debate, the Training Department was boldly renamed the Department of Arts, Science and Education. (That was surely an academy in which Leonardo would have found a niche.) And thanks to the generosity of the Goldsmiths' Company, there were actually, for a few years, Professors of Education working in the department: James Britton (1970-5) and Maurice Craft (1976-9).

In 1976, an internal reorganisation of the College led to the creation of a School of Education, with Mr A. V. Kelly as its Dean. It had to operate in a very different world from its predecessor, the DASE. A series of DES circulars following on the publication of a government White Paper in December 1972 – inappropriately entitled 'Education: A Framework for Expansion' – enforced on the Colleges of Education a sudden and drastic reduction in the number of students the DES would allow to be trained as teachers. (Earlier predictions about the

122

123

122 C. W. Green,
long-serving Lecturer in
History, later Vice-Principal
and acting Warden in 1975.

123 Teaching practice,
1983.

124 A seminar in the
Education building.

124

national birthrate had proved to be quite wrong). The numbers
were to be halved by 1980. There followed the wholesale closure
of colleges and amalgamations between others. Goldsmiths'
was directly affected by all this in two major ways. First of all,
under strong pressure from the DES, it was decided that two
local colleges should be joined with Goldsmiths' to create a
substantially larger institution. They were St Gabriel's in
Camberwell, a Church of England College founded in 1868, and
Rachel McMillan College in Deptford, an ILEA college for the
training of primary school teachers, founded in 1930 by
Margaret McMillan. Needless to say, these amalgamations were

125

125 Professor A. V. Kelly,
Dean of the School of
Education 1976-87, Dean of
the Faculty of Education
1987-, appointed by the
University to a personal
chair in curriculum studies
February 1989.

126 Design and Technology
students at work.

126

complicated affairs. There were legal problems to be overcome
and problems also of administration, staffing and finance. A
special committee, the 'Formation Committee', under the
chairmanship of Professor K. W. Keohane, Rector of the
Roehampton Institute of Higher Education, was appointed to
handle them, and the amalgamations were formally held to have

127 More teaching practice.

been completed on 1 August 1977, having first been mooted some four years earlier.

However, the problems were not all resolved by the simple declaration that they had been. The numerical problems posed by this sudden reversal of government policy were extremely severe. The number of student places which had, in 1970, been filled by education students at Goldsmiths' and the other two colleges had to be halved, to about 1000, by 1980. As will be seen, the College used the number of student places thus 'freed' to increase greatly the number of undergraduates following other courses. But the School of Education itself had quickly to branch out in other directions. In particular, there was a rapid increase in postgraduate work and a considerable extension of in-service courses for practising teachers. The School also had to give constant thought to the form of the B Ed degree. There was a long-running debate as to whether this course should be devoted exclusively to educational subjects or whether it should combine these with other classroom subjects. On the whole, the educationalists, not surprisingly, wanted a degree course which concentrated pretty well totally on educational or professional matters and the third version of the degree provided for just that. But during the 1980s, there was increasing government intervention in the training of teachers, and pressure for a sort of joint degree became irresistible. So, at the time of writing, a fourth version is being devised.

128

129

128 Before the one-way
system, a view from 1950.

129 The New Cross
Kinema, opened in 1925 and
closed in 1960.

15 Adult Studies

In 1965, the Evening Department was renamed the Adult Studies Department, and it is perhaps not fanciful to regard this as marking a considerable change of emphasis in its work. Flexibility had always been necessary: there was no point in putting on courses which nobody wanted to attend, and quick response to demand was essential if numbers were to be kept up and required services provided. From the early 1960s, a clear demand for more advanced work began to be noticeable, while at the same time a major reorganisation being carried out by the LCC of its own evening institutes exposed the Department to the risk that it would find itself engaged in fruitless competition for customers for less advanced courses and activities. Eventually, after great and anxious debate within the Department and the College, with the LCC and with HMIs, it was decided that the Department, from the autumn of 1964, should begin to run a part-time degree course in Sociology.

This was a major policy change. Hitherto, evening institutes had been chary of making any clear distinction between educational and recreational activities, and they eschewed work which was primarily vocational. Also they had left degree teaching strictly to the Universities. But the demand existed, and the success of the new policy was dramatic. By 1968, there were 156 full-time undergraduates and 242 part-time undergraduates reading for degrees in Sociology, Psychology and Music; also a small number of postgraduate students. There was a sharp increase in the number of students studying for four-year Diploma courses; preparatory courses for Open University programmes were now being mounted; and in 1971 a graduate course in Applied Social Studies was begun.

These developments were not achieved without difficulty. In the earlier years, when the Department was still being financed by the ILEA, staff appointments had to be negotiated with that body and these negotiations were not always easy. There were serious problems of accommodation, where the Department was necessarily in competition with the constantly expanding DASE. It is clear that Ian Gulland came to feel that he was not always fairly treated in this matter by the College authorities, though George Wood, the Registrar, was a keen supporter. Peter Bindley, Gulland's deputy, wrote later of Wood's enthus-

130 An expedition by the
Evening Students
Association Rambling Club.

131 Goldsmiths' College
and south-east London.

130

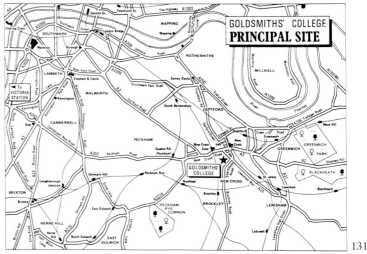

131

iasm for 'purchasing or renting houses across the road for the
College or in the surrounding terraces. He was rather like a
keen Monopoly player: if he got three houses together on the
board we could have a Sociology Department.'

However, these developments of advanced work by no
means put an end to the old Liberal Studies programmes which
continued to attract an annual enrolment of well over 4000
persons, though there was, certainly, some falling off in social
and recreational activities. But, during the 1970s and early
1980s, there was a definite change of emphasis in the direction
of community education, exemplified by the establishment of
a Community Education Centre at Lee Green in 1973, and the
Turning Point scheme in 1980, by which the Department
undertook a systematic training programme for adults already
active in community work of various kinds. A two-year course

132 Malcolm Barry, Dean of the School of Adult and Community Studies 1985-7 and Director of Continuing Education since 1987.

133 A Turning-Point community work apprentice working with a Pensioners' Group on a south London council estate.

for Community and Youth workers had started as early as 1970. It was in that year that Peter Baynes succeeded Gulland as Principal of the Adult Studies Department.

He became, in 1976, as a result of an internal College reorganisation, Dean of the School of Adult and Social Studies, though his successor, Colin Titmus (1981-5) inherited only part of his empire, as a result of the creation of a new School of Social Sciences, in which were based all the Social Sciences Departments engaged in degree teaching. This change marked the return to the pattern that had obtained before 1964, but it certainly did not stem from any feeling that it had been a mistake for degree work to have been started in the Evening Department. It was rather that the academic purposes and practices of the different sections of the School were so different, particularly with the growth of community education work, that they no longer sat very easily together in one organisation.

As will be shown later, the strengths of the School of Adult and Community Studies and of its multifarious activities were to be an important factor in the later upturn in the College's constitutional fortunes. But the evening programme as a whole was notable for another reason. It gave the College a very special social character. In not a few university institutions, a great silence descends in the late afternoon as the undergraduates make off to their flats or hostels, or even local hostelries; lecture-rooms are deserted, corridors emptied, common-rooms and dining-rooms disused. In Goldsmiths', a great new burst of activity begins as scores, even hundreds, of evening students pour in to take up their various activities. It is a circumstance which enabled the College to claim with justice that it makes exceptionally good use of its plant.

134 Patrick Ferguson
Millard, Principal of the
School of Art 1958-67.
Portrait head by Ivor Roberts
Jones, a lecturer at the
School of Art and a
distinguished sculptor.

16 The School of Art from 1958

Clive Gardiner retired as Principal in July 1958. His successor, Patrick Millard, was an experienced teacher and a landscape painter of some note. He drew his inspiration particularly from his native Cumbria and the wilder regions of Wales and northern England. But he was not able, as a later Principal wrote of Gardiner, 'to lead the School from behind the easel rather than the desk' for he was immediately confronted by formidable administrative and professional problems. Reports from the National Advisory Council on Art Education proposed a complete new structure for art school courses. Briefly, it suggested a one-year pre-diploma course, to be followed by a three-year diploma course of degree standard. The main subjects in this new Diploma in Art and Design were to be painting, sculpture, illustration and textile/fashion. A new National Council for Diplomas in Art and Design was established in 1961 under the chairmanship of Sir John Summerson, charged with vetting proposals from the art schools for diploma courses on the new model. Great carnage followed. In all, 87 colleges submitted proposals for 201 different courses. Only 61 of these courses were approved from just 28 institutions.

The Summerson Council, which was to evolve into the Council for National Academic Awards, made its decisions on the basis of reports of visitations made by panels of experts. These visitations were extremely searching and Goldsmiths' emerged from them with great credit, securing approval for its painting and sculpture diploma courses in 1962 and for its textile/embroidery courses in the following year. These courses were rechristened BA courses in 1975. Other degree courses have been established since then, such as a combined degree in Communication Study and Sociology, a number of postgraduate degrees such as a part-time MA course in Fine Art and a joint degree in Art and Art History.

A certain amount of non-degree work survived, and of course still survives. All the same, the College's success in obtaining validation for its new courses – a success which owed a great deal to the meticulous care with which Millard prepared for the original visitations of the Summerson Council – brought about a fundamental change in the character and purpose of the school's work. As has been shown, the majority of students in

135 Patrick Ferguson
Millard, Dufton Pike,
Westmorland.
Watercolour 20 x 32 cms.

136 Peter de Francia,
Principal of the School of Art
1969 - 72, Nude.
Painting in oils 24 x 18 in.

137 H. Thubron, Corridor.
74 x 86 cms.

138 Work in progress in the
Ceramics building, 1982.

135

136

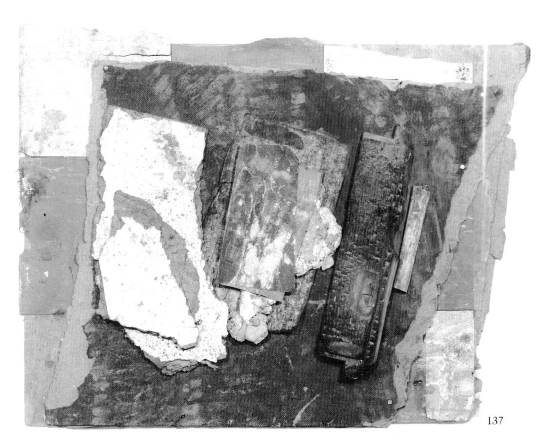

137

138

139 Peter MacKarell, Aixe-sur-Vienne 1984.
Watercolour 17 x 12½ in.

140 Basil Beattie, Legend 1986.
8ft 6in x 12in.

141 Peter Cresswell, Dean of the School of Art and Design 1984-7, Dean of the Faculty of Arts 1987-.

139

Gardiner's time took no examinations at all. Now the great majority of them read for first or second degrees, like students in other areas of the College. This change was marked by the creation in 1987 of a new Faculty of Arts, which includes the Humanities departments as well as all those dealing with the creative and performing arts.

Millard and his successors had to face one extremely difficult problem. For ten years before 1974, negotiations were carried on with the Inner London Education Authority for the erection of a new School of Art building on the main site. Pending its construction the authority was understandably reluctant to incur expenditure on conversions of other buildings, or on temporary accommodation. The CNAA in its periodic reports on the College's courses was frequently highly critical of the accommodation it provided, and the school faced a serious crisis with the cancellation of the new building project in 1974. To some extent, the problem was solved when the College acquired St Gabriel's College in Camberwell and was able to make use of the building to house a large part of the School of Art until space became available on the main site in 1988, as a result of the building of the new College library.

There have continued to be artists of great note working in the College since Gardiner's time. Many readers will be familiar with the massive statue of Churchill by Ivor Roberts Jones which broods so glumly over Parliament Square. Kenneth Martin, Bert Irvin, Michael Craig-Martin, Mike Kenny and Basil Beattie are other familiar names and the works of several Goldsmiths' artists are represented in the College's collection. But there did not emerge any single group exactly comparable with the Goldsmiths' school of the 1920s. This may be due to the prevailing philosophy of the school. To a large extent, students in the area of fine art are expected to design their own

140

141

courses in consultation with their tutors, and the modern degree course is not sub-divided according to the traditional categories of practice, painting, sculpture and printmaking. In the words of a recent chairman of the Visual Arts department 'it sees fine art as a broad field of inter-disciplinary practice, within which students are required, under tutorial guidance, to find and develop their own points of differentiation'.

The period since 1970 has, however, firmly established Goldsmiths' as a leader in the field of Fine Art practice. No longer just an interesting alternative to the Central London schools, the College is widely regarded as the most successful participant on the world stage of any of the UK's Fine Art departments. It is significant that in the British Art Show for 1990, which featured forty artists under thirty-five years of age selected from a national entry of 2,800, no fewer than thirteen of those exhibiting had studied at Goldsmiths'.

The College offers a slightly more specialised degree course in textiles. Embroidery was traditionally appreciated just for skilful decorative techniques, but Constance Howard who came to work in Goldsmiths' in 1947 was one of a small number of artists who developed the notion of embroidery as an art form

142

143

142 Albert Irvin, Sandy
Mount II 1987.
Acrylic on canvas,
152 x 183 cms.

143 Michael Kenny RA,
Americium, I, 1988.
Relief-oil paint on wood.
188 (height) x 213.5 x 23.5
cms.

144 Melanie Williams,
Little Bo Peep.
PapierMâché and hand
embroidery, 18 x 12½ in.

145 Post-graduate film
students on location in
Scotland, filming a scene
from *Shona May*,
Goldsmiths' prize-winning
entry to the Fuji Film
scholarship, shown on
Thames Television in 1988.

144

145

146 First-year
Communication students on
a 'Press Trip' to the City
Airport as part of their
introduction to a Journalism
Course, 1989.

and as a vehicle for artistic self-expression. The present degree, with its great diversity in the application of textiles practice, evolved from the diploma course which began in 1964 and very largely reflected her ideas. The Art Teacher's Certificate course, though actually located in the Faculty of Education since 1983, has continued to thrive. A number of experts in the area of art education worked with the course, including Robert Brazil and Anton Ehrenzweig. And there was much sadness in the College when the head of the course, Dr Peter MacKarell, died in 1988 at the early age of fifty-four.

The Faculty of Arts will have undergone one other great change by 1991. The admission of the College as a School of the University will mean that from then on, all its degree students will be reading for University of London degrees. So the visual arts department will be more fully integrated with the work of the rest of the College than it has been since the days of the Goldsmiths' Institute.

17 The Murray Report

147 Professor E. H. Warmington, eighth Chairman of the Delegacy 1958-75, Hon Fellow 1975, Professor of Classics at Birkbeck College 1935-65. Portrait in oils by John Mansbridge.

Early in 1963, before the publication of the Robbins Report, a meeting was held between the Chairman of the Delegacy, the Warden, and the Principal of the University, to discuss the College's future. It was not an encouraging meeting for the College, as the Principal, Sir Douglas Logan, made it plain that he did not expect it to be given an improved status within the University, which had itself become so large and diffuse that strong attempts were being made to make it more compact and to reduce its peripheral activities. Not surprisingly, though, the Robbins Report, with its fundamental recommendations that higher education should be greatly expanded and that six new Universities be quickly founded, stirred the College into fresh activity. For the first time for many years, the idea of the College becoming an independent University of South London was canvassed. On 26 November 1963, the Delegacy resolved unanimously that 'the aim of Goldsmiths' College should be to achieve University status as an independent institution'.

This bold declaration, however, came to nothing. Further meetings at Senate House led members of the Delegacy to become daunted by the complexities of achieving total independence and convinced them that the College's long-term interests would still be best served by developing its connections with the University of London. On the other hand, it became plain that there was no chance of the College becoming a School in the near future. The process of making new financial arrangements would have been an extremely difficult one and as, following the Robbins Report, the University was having to undertake a major review of its own arrangements, it would not be willing to increase the number of Schools until that review had been completed. So, the College was, so to speak, stymied. A number of important changes of the kind recommended by Robbins were carried through in London. Others ran into legal difficulties, and so, in 1970, a Committee of Enquiry into the governance of the University was set up jointly by the University and the UGC, under the chairmanship of Lord Murray of Newhaven.

The College had no option but to await its findings. At times, the possibility of its leaving the University sector altogether and getting itself set up as an independent institution in the public

148 After the Library fire, 1971.

sector – a sort of Polytechnic – teaching for degrees validated by the recently founded Council for National Academic Awards, was considered. But·there was never much enthusiasm for this option: the historical and academic links with the University were still much valued, and University status, in some form or other, remained the College's prime object.

In its submission to the Murray Enquiry the College made it plain that it hoped in the long run to become an independent University, but that it believed that this object could be best achieved if it first became a School of London University.

There seems to have been some incompatibility between these two objectives. The first would, presumably, have involved the severance of traditional academic links between the College and the University; the second would, at least in the short run, have strengthened them. Also, since the University had several times made it clear that it was concerned about the amount of administrative work that would have been involved in turning Goldsmiths' into a School, it may have been unwise for the College to expect the University to undertake this, simply to provide it with a sort of staging-post on the road to full independence.

All the same, the College had high hopes of the Murray

149

149 Professor R. O. Buchanan, Professor of Geography at the London School of Economics and member of the Delegacy 1954-80. Portrait in oils by John Mansbridge.

150 Mr J. L. Coleman, Bursar until 1984, and Mr W. H. Jones, formerly Academic Registrar, in February 1984.

Enquiry. Those who met the members of the committee when they visited the College late in 1970 thought the occasion had gone very promisingly and the final report, published in the autumn of 1972, came as a bad blow. It agreed that the College should be given an independent legal status, but did not believe that its admission as a School would be of advantage either to the University or to the College itself. It took the view that the College was 'still fundamentally a teacher training institution'; and that its future would have to depend on future decisions by the government. But the committee also recommended the complete phasing out of the IRT system, by which students at external institutions could read for London degrees. The implementation of these recommendations would itself have terminated the College's academic connection with the University. The Murray Enquiry's conclusion with regard to the College's future was perhaps a shade perfunctory. 'While there are other possible directions in which the College might move on becoming independent and ending its present form of association with the University of London, we do not think we are the right or the competent body to choose between them'. The University moved rapidly to end the IRT system. Colleges of Education formerly grouped together in the Institute of Education passed to the public sector, under the academic control of the CNAA. But the University did not act on the recommendation that Goldsmiths' should join the exodus, so it retained, for a further sixteen years, its anomalous status, as much the largest of a much shrunken band of Institutions with Recognised Teachers.

150

151 Geology students doing
field work on Skye. The
Cuillins are in the
background.

18 The Great Change

While the government was pursuing policies on teacher training which would surely have attracted the admiring respect of the Grand Old Duke of York, a great change was happening in the College. As has been shown, the Evening Department had decided to break with its own traditions and begin to teach for University degree courses, starting with a part-time degree in sociology in 1964. In time this development was to bring about a transformation of almost the whole College.

Since the closure of the old Science Department in 1915, students who had read for London University degrees had combined this work with the Certificate of Education course. They had been aspiring teachers, happy to acquire a further academic and professional qualification. The numbers of students following these combined courses increased greatly during the 1960s. But, with the sociology degree, followed very shortly by psychology and music degrees, the College was for the first time teaching for degrees for, so to speak, their own sake. French and German soon followed the example of sociology and, by the mid-1970s, all the rest of the College had followed suit. By then, it was teaching for a range of degree courses wider than that offered by some of the Schools of the University, and indeed by a number of independent universities. True, there was no classics or law; no philosophy or economics; no engineering or medicine. But there was history, English, drama, music, French, German, geography and religion; sociology, social science and administration, psychology, social anthropology; mathematics, physics, chemistry, geology, botany and zoology. Also, by 1979, the Certificate of Education course was being phased out, with the result that almost all education students other than those engaged in postgraduate work were reading for the B Ed degree. Degree courses were also being mounted in the School of Art, under the auspices of the CNAA.

A few figures will demonstrate the magnitude of this change. In the academic year 1970-1, 1967 students were undergoing some form of teacher training. Of these, 452 were taking the four-year combined course, 62 were reading for the B Ed degree, and 216 were taking the one-year postgraduate course. In that year, 82 students graduated with degrees in sociology, music or

152 George Cecil Wood,
first Registrar of the College
1958-77.

psychology. And, in the School of Art, 154 students were studying for the Diploma in Art and Design. But 1237 students, by far the largest single group and a majority of the whole, were still engaged on the three-year Certificate of Education course.

Ten years later, the position was very different. Almost 1600 students were reading for first degrees in subjects other than education, and almost 200 for higher degrees. There were 224 students in the School of Art who were studying for CNAA degrees. The three-year certificate course was being phased out and the great majority of students undergoing initial teacher training were reading for the B Ed degree. The training of teachers was still an important part of the College's activities, but it was no longer the College's chief purpose and it was no longer true, as it had been at the time of the Murray Enquiry that Goldsmiths' was 'still fundamentally a Teacher Training Institution'.

It is important to stress that all this happened at the behest of the DES, and was indeed imposed on the College by the Department's insistence that the student places made available following the amalgamation with St Gabriel's and Rachel McMillan Colleges should be filled by students taking degree courses in subjects other than education. It also had, in so far as was necessary, the approbation of the ILEA; and was within the knowledge of Her Majesty's Inspectors and sundry other official bodies. Furthermore, it had the approval of the University of London, for every new proposal to teach for a London degree had to obtain the support of the relevant Board of Studies and the approval of the University's Academic Council. There were great complications, because of the restrictions imposed by the Senate on the ability of Institutions with Recognised Teachers to extend their range of degree courses and because, from 1972, the whole IRT system was in dissolution. But it is not intended to give any further account of the prolonged discussions that took place on these matters; the important point is that the University knew what was happening and permitted it.

However, it is true also that these changes occurred, not indeed by stealth but certainly by stages, and it may be wondered whether their magnitude and significance was fully grasped. (Though few can have been so out of touch with them as the retired politician who once astounded the company at a Goldsmiths' College Association Dinner by assuring it that the filigree work of Goldsmiths' College students was widely esteemed throughout the Commonwealth.)

To take the position of the DES first. Daunted by a great tide of applications from cities and towns all over the kingdom, it announced˙ very soon after the appearance of the Robbins Report that no new Universities were to be set up for at least

153 Stanley Glasser, Head of the Music Department from 1969, Dean of the School of Humanities and Performing Arts 1977-83 appointed by the University to a personal chair in Music October 1989.

154 Alan Little, Lewisham Professor of Social Administration 1977-86.

ten years. Yet there is a sense in which it allowed something rather like that to happen at New Cross, in that the College was producing, each year, several hundred honours graduates of the University of London with degrees in subjects other than Education. Moreover, a new financial and constitutional anomaly was created, made the more odd when the DES reached an agreement with the ILEA in 1977 progressively to take over financial responsibility for the School of Art and the Adult Studies Department. With the exception of the Open University, the Cranfield Institute of Technology, and a small number of single-subject institutions, all English and Welsh Universities received their funds from the University Grants Committee, and the size of these grants was determined by the academic judgement of that body. But Goldsmiths' College received its grant direct from government, and the UGC had no financial responsibility for, and so no policy-making control over, the College.

The University of London, also, had landed itself with a problem it may not have quite foreseen. This stemmed from the decision made by the Senate in 1965 that the College should have restored to it the right to teach for internal degrees of the University. For the previous fifteen years, Goldsmiths' College students had been reading for the University's external degrees in the same way as private students from other non-university institutions all over the country and indeed the world; but in 1972 the University had terminated the rights of students in public educational institutions to register for these examinations. Goldsmiths' was now an exception. The Sen-

155 The main site of the College, September 1987.

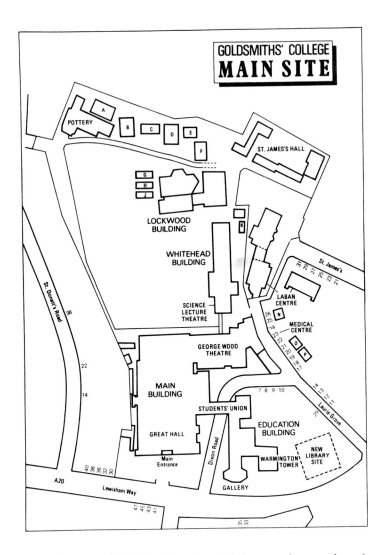

ate's decision of 1965 had been hedged about with a number of regulations which the College was to find increasingly inhibiting. But without it, its massive expansion into degree teaching could not have occurred.

It would not be easy, and might be invidious to identify individuals who were particularly active in carrying through these changes. Getting started on teaching for degree courses had to be a sort of team effort, in that Heads of Departments and their colleagues had not only to make their case to the College, but also to convince the relevant University Board of Studies that the department had the necessary resources, teaching space and academic strength to do the job properly. All the same, two individuals will be mentioned here. R. A. Pinker was appointed to a lectureship in sociology in 1964 with specific responsibility for the part-time degree course in sociology, which recruited its first students that autumn. He pioneered the route that many of his colleagues were to follow and became, in 1972, the first Lewisham Professor of Social Administration. It was a Chair unique in Britain in that it was funded by a local authority and it seems right gratefully to salute the generosity of the London Borough of Lewisham. Pinker moved in 1975 to a Chair in Chelsea College and was succeeded the following year by Alan Little. Until his tragically early death, Little was a major force in College affairs. Indeed, his success as a scholar and academic leader, and his commitment to public affairs, demonstrated all too clearly how much the College suffered from the prohibition imposed by the University, shortly after his appointment, on its being able to engage the services of other Professors or Readers.

Not all the changes described above occurred without pain or difficulty, and some projects foundered altogether, like those for economics and part-time language degrees. There were difficulties in the early years, particularly over staff appointments and accommodation, partly arising from the fact that the Adult Studies Department was financed by the ILEA, and the criteria it adopted were not always the same as those employed by the DES. There were continuing problems, also, arising from the fact that quite a number of teaching staff, who had originally been appointed to the Training Department, or St Gabriel's and Rachel McMillan Colleges, were not suited by taste or talent for teaching in departments chiefly concerned in preparing undergraduates and postgraduates for University degrees in subjects other than education. All the same, it was a considerable achievement that these changes were carried through so successfully in a relatively short period that, in 1986 and 1987, the University of London and the University Grants Committee were satisfied, after searching enquiries, that the academic work of Goldsmiths' College was actually or potentially on a par with that of other long-established Schools of the University.

156 H. Mackenzie, New
Cross 1981.
Watercolour, 32 x 45 cms.

19 Administration and Government

157 Dr Richard Hoggart, seventh Warden of the College 1976-84, Hon Fellow 1987. Portrait in oils by Peter Cresswell.

Inevitably, the growth of the College and the increasing complexity of its activities resulted in a great increase in the amount of administrative work to be done and the number of administrators employed to do it. Gone were the days when it could mostly be left to two jovial brothers working behind locked doors and wearing bowler hats. (Though there are still reactionary persons about who sometimes wonder whether things would be all that less efficient if letters still had to be written in long-hand and if modern processes of duplication and computation did not so easily produce such burdensome quantities of documents.) As early as 1968, a firm of management consultants was commissioned to make a report on the College's administrative structures. One of their criticisms was that the Registrar himself had too much to do:

At present no fewer than fifteen administrative and clerical officers report directly to the Registrar. These officers are of varying ranks, with the result that the Registrar is constantly being interrupted to deal with a whole range of minor problems, many of which should, in our opinion, have been settled at subordinate level.

This was not a surprising conclusion for there were ways in which George Wood was not the very model of a modern civil servant. He overworked constantly, took no exercise and very few holidays, and found it difficult to delegate authority. He did not maintain much in the way of a filing system, apart from those papers he took home each night in four bulging briefcases. There were occasions, after his sadly early death, when the College was surprised by the appearance of awkward documents, relating to contracts of employment, conveyances and the like, of which it had no record. Yet he was undoubtedly one of the great figures in College history; was always anxious to get things done; and was far more readily excited by new opportunities than daunted by obstacles. Warden Hoggart referred to his 'creative untidiness'. He did everything he could to carry through the major changes that occurred in his time, and indeed inspired not a few of them. He was extremely successful in establishing good relations with the DES, the ILEA and the London Borough of Lewisham; relations which were, on occasion, to be of great political and financial advantage to the College. He was also a quite exceptionally nice man

158

159

160

and, after his death, the College commemorated him by giving his name to the Theatre and commissioning James Sutton to make the elegant plaque which hangs in the foyer. His successor, S. D. (Pip) Leedam (1978-86), carried on his work, though his time and energy had often to be given to organising and preparing for the endless series of meetings which had, during his years, to be held upon the College's financial and constitutional problems. Shane Guy came from Liverpool University in 1987 to succeed Leedam. Barry Tait took over from Jack Coleman as Finance Officer in 1983.

The Governing Body was enlarged, perhaps to an unmanageable degree, during these years. Two or three of its members were particularly important. E. H. Warmington, Professor of Classics at Birkbeck College, was Chairman from 1958 to 1975, and R. O. Buchanan, Professor of Geography at the London School of Economics, was a member from 1954 until his death in 1980. It is doubtful whether any Chairman ever gave so much time and thought to College affairs as Warmington did, and he and Buchanan played a quite crucial role in keeping the sometimes difficult relations between the College and the University on a reasonably even keel. None of those who saw it will forget Warmington's brave appearance, when already a very old man, at an Honorary Fellowship Ceremony in February 1984, and Buchanan was, right up to his death, a familiar figure in College, readily identified by his merry smile and twinkling eyes, his remarkable wide-brimmed hats and strange habit of always running up and down stairs. Mention should also be made of C. P. de B. Jenkins, Clerk to the Goldsmiths' Company and member of the delegacy from 1970 to 1988 and thereafter of the Council. His robust and sceptical commonsense often served to keep the imagination of some colleagues in contact with the realities of the modern world.

Ross Chesterman became Warden in 1953, having previously been the Headmaster of a school at Southport, and then Chief County Inspector of Schools for Worcestershire. As has been shown, he was fortunate in the quality of many of his senior colleagues, people like Wood, Millard and Gulland. He was to be bitterly disappointed by the findings of the Murray Enquiry, which appeared at the time to have erected a quite unexpected obstacle to what seemed to be the natural future development of the College. For it was Chesterman who presided, equably and calmly, over the great change and it was very largely due to him that it was accomplished without causing too much stress, anxiety, or disharmony within the College. He played a key role in discussions with the University about the first version of the B Ed degree, and formulated with great clarity many of the policies and strategies the College followed in subsequent years.

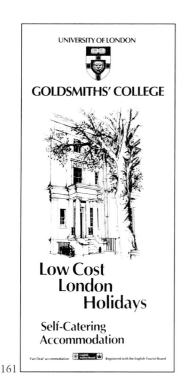

UNIVERSITY OF LONDON

GOLDSMITHS' COLLEGE

Low Cost
London
Holidays

Self-Catering
Accommodation

'Fair Deal' accommodation   Registered with the English Tourist Board

161

158 Lord Perry of Walton
(left), eleventh Chairman of
the Delegacy 1981-4, and
Founding Vice-Chancellor of
the Open University,
receiving a farewell gift from
the Delegacy, a watercolour
by Peter MacKarell, from the
Vice-Chairman, C. P. de B.
Jenkins, 16 October 1984.

159 S. J. (Pip) Leedam,
second Registrar of the
College 1978-86.

160 B. W. Tait, Finance
Officer and Deputy Registrar
from 1983.

161 Holiday
accommodation leaflet. Like
many similar institutions
the College tries to make
money from vacation
lettings of its properties.

His successor, F. M. G. Willson (1974-5), did not have time
to make a great impression on the College; he succeeded Sir
Douglas Logan as Principal of London University just a year
after becoming Warden. And it is not easy to write about his
successor, Richard Hoggart, as the author regards him as one of
his closest friends; his memory is still fresh in College and, of
course, he is still an active public figure. But one or two points
must at least be made. He was, as a result of his own exper-
iences, perhaps uniquely qualified to lead and represent an
institution as diverse as Goldsmiths'. He had started his career
as a lecturer in adult education, had held a Chair at Birming-
ham University, and came to the College after a number of
years as a Deputy Director of UNESCO. During his time as
Warden, he served as Vice-Chairman of the Arts Council of
Great Britain and Chairman of the Advisory Council on Adult
Education. He was the author of a famous book *The Uses of
Literacy*. As no previous Warden had been in a position to do,
he was able to put, and keep, the College in the public eye, or
on the academic map. Also, at times when the College's affairs
were not always going too well, he was absolutely, and always,
unwilling to admit defeat.

These later Wardens presided over a system of government
vastly more elaborate than their predecessors had done. It is
not proposed to give a blow by blow account of all the changes
that were made. By 1970, the earlier dearth of College committees had been amply compensated for, though it must be
said that the committee structure of that year bore the same
sort of relation to its ultimate flowering in 1976 as a crisp early
Haydn symphony does to the complexities of one of Mahler's
more ample works. By 1970, each constituent department of
the College had its own Academic Board and each of them was
well furnished with subsidiary bodies. For example: in the
Department of Arts, Science and Education, the Certificate of
Education and B Ed Courses Committee was served by four
sub-committees. There was a Postgraduate Courses Commit-
tee, a Resources Committee, a Research Committee, a Staffing
Committee, a Promotions Committee; there was a Library
Committee, a Joint Refectory Committee, a College Shop
Committee, a Technical Aids Committee, a Public Lectures
Committee, a Safety Committee and a Medical Committee.
There were regular faculty meetings and a Board of Faculties
which had, no doubt necessarily, a co-ordinating function.
There was a Staff Council, on which all teaching members of
the Department were entitled to sit. There was a College
Executive Committee. It was pointed out by Cyril Green, then
Deputy Principal, that this singular structure did not make for
speedy decision-making.

162

163

The chief change made in 1976 was that there was to be one single Academic Board and that all departments and academic activities were parcelled out among five separate schools, each provided with its own Dean and its own Board of Studies. A sixth school was added in 1980 when the School of Adult and Social Studies was divided into two. There is no doubt that the object of this change, the creation of a single Academic Board and parallel subsidiary bodies, was to integrate more closely the diverse activities of the College. For many years in the past, successive Wardens had been claiming that the Training Department, the School of Art and the Evening Department had been working together ever more harmoniously, but the very frequency with which this was asserted makes it a shade doubtful whether the claim had always been well founded, or at least makes one suspect that the earlier cacophony must have been deafening indeed. But the 1976 scheme did not entirely achieve this objective. For the purposes of the allocation of resources, the new schools quickly organised themselves into something like feudal armies and the Chairman of a College Committee charged with the allocation of academic accommodation once ruefully reminded his colleagues of a saying of a one-time Chancellor of the Austro-Hungarian Empire: 'It is the policy of the government of His Imperial and Apostolic Majesty to maintain the subject peoples of his empire in a state of balanced and equal discontent'.

The new systems of the 1960s and 1970s were meant to enshrine the fashionable principles of consultation and participation, the more so as, for the first time, extensive provision was made for formal student representation on College committees and for consultative committees with the recognised trade unions. And there is no doubt that, unless pretty well the whole College had felt itself to be involved in the carrying through of the great change, it could hardly have happened. All the same, the plans did not quite work. Great amounts of time were spent, and possibly wasted, when the same subjects were debated, over and over again, sometimes by the same people wearing different hats, in a great number of parallel or overlapping committees. But, more important, the new systems could not produce quick results and, all too often, crises arose, deadlines were set, decisions had to be made, which did not allow of punctilious observance of the College's official constitution. Early in March 1980, for instance, the DES unexpectedly informed the Bursar that it found itself able to make an extra half a million pounds available to the College, provided it was spent within about three weeks. The Warden and the Deans quickly decided that much of this money should be spent on the purchase of new library books. There was no time

162 Dr Doreen Asso, Dean of the Faculty of Social and Mathematical Sciences from 1986.

163 Shane Guy, third Registrar and first Secretary of the College from 1987.

164 Small houses in streets near the College provide useful offices for teachers and administrators.

to decide exactly what each department was entitled to, or should spend; instead, members of the academic and library staff rushed off to Dillon's, or Hatchard's, or Blackwell's with Gladstone bags or haversacks to buy up whatever they thought appropriate. But, more gravely, it happened on a number of occasions in the 1980s that the College learnt – very late in the academic year – that it was going to have much less money in the following year than it had hoped for. Again, there was no time to crank the whole cumbrous system up. Instead Wardens Hoggart and Rutherford had to establish ad hoc working parties to make, at very short notice, the cuts that were necessary to protect the College from financial disaster.

By 1986, the defects of the system had become obvious to all and there was yet another major internal reorganisation, initiated by the new Warden in response to the Jarratt Report on Efficiency in Universities. The six schools were compressed into three faculties, the number of individual departments was reduced by a series of amalgamations, the Governing Body and the Academic Board were cut down in size, and a new, more streamlined committee system was devised. The object of these changes was to ensure that decisions could be made reasonably quickly and that the processes of consultation and participation would actually work. Those, of course, have been the objectives constitution makers have set themselves over the centuries. Only time will tell whether the new system achieves them, but thus far it has worked reasonably well.

165 An undergraduate room
at Pentland House.

20 Modern College Life

In Goldsmiths' as in all other universities and colleges, conditions of life have changed radically over the last twenty or thirty years. Gone are most of the formal college occasions, the morning assembly, the mid-day dinner, the Foundation Oration. No gowns are to be seen, no Latin graces heard. Many of the festive functions have lapsed also. There is no College Sports Day, no official ball; the School of Art no longer makes it its business to entertain the rest of the College at the end of the summer term. The Senior Common Room has fallen into a sad decline, and the Goldsmiths' College Association has found it increasingly difficult to attract new members. Rules and regulations have been relaxed to a degree Loring or Dean would have found incredible, and the official segregation of the sexes has long since gone. Only the longest surviving members of staff can confidently remember which was the men's, and which the women's corridor. In short, most of the aspects of college life which were perhaps more like those of a boarding-school have simply vanished.

These and similar changes occurred for three main reasons. Firstly, the growth in numbers meant that, for example, there was nowhere where all the staff and students could eat even a modest meal together. Secondly, the diversification of academic activity meant that staff and students were engaged on many different things. In earlier days, the social coherence of the training department derived largely from the fact that the students were all following the same courses, under the same teachers. And, thirdly, winds of change, blowing in from almost every point of the compass, swept away many assumptions and conventions which had stood unchallenged for decades.

Some good things were lost. For one thing, the staff became far too large for everyone to know one another. The College authorities inevitably became more remote figures, and a certain tetchiness manifested itself in College life, induced perhaps by constitutional and financial anxieties, perhaps by memories of the student 'stirs' of the late 1960s – though Goldsmiths' was spared any dramatic manifestations of the student revolt – most probably by the impact of general social and political concerns and divisions. But there were still cakes

166 The Staff Cricket XI at Loring Hall, summer 1985.

167 In the Students' Union bar.

168 Sunday evening Mass at the Roman Catholic Chaplaincy.

169 The Electronic Music Studio, November 1985.

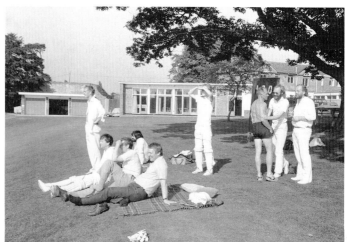

166

167

and ale; social life in the departments themselves flourished; and who am I to say that discos in the Students' Union are not just as much fun as the white-tie balls of earlier years? And if, largely for financial reasons, the College has had to abandon its policy of providing places in Halls of Residence for all its students – some of the smaller hostels, including Loring Hall, have been given up, and Grove Hall had to be sold to help pay for the new Library – many modern students much prefer to fend for themselves anyway. In fact the College did acquire two large halls of residence in Camberwell and one in Deptford at the time of the amalgamation, and is still able to provide a higher proportion of places in college hostels than most other colleges of the University.

A more fundamental change was that, having been a Teacher Training College attached to a University, it became a University institution in its own right, a change which was marked, not made, by its becoming a School. The academic

168

169

standards of its students have undoubtedly been raised, partly, no doubt, as a result of the Education Act of 1944, and partly because, in recent years, pretty well all the students have had to have the qualifications necessary for reading for degrees. But the diversification of its academic activities, and the fact that it is now teaching almost exclusively for undergraduate and postgraduate courses, in education as elsewhere, has made it both necessary and possible to recruit members of staff with different and perhaps higher academic qualifications and achievements. Also, the College has been able to obtain some major research grants, for example, for the assessment of performance in Design and Technology in schools, and for mon-

170 Gala Day, June 1986.

171 The Spring Ball at Dean Hall, 1987.

172 Climbing practice.

173 Undergraduates at the Laban Centre rehearsing in one of the studios carved out of St James's Church.

174 Students reading Modern Languages spend a year of their course abroad. These students were photographed in front of a memorial to D'Artagnan at Toulouse-le-Mirail.

170

171

itoring needle-exchange schemes for drug users. Dr Paul Steinitz OBE (1909-88), might serve as a particularly good example of the sort of scholar the College has been able to attract in recent years. One of the world's greatest authorities on the music of Bach and its performance, the Founder of the London Bach Society and the Steinitz Bach Players, he worked as a lecturer in the College Music Department from 1968, just at the time when it embarked on degree teaching, until 1980. His greatest feat was his directing performances of all the Bach Cantatas, an extraordinary project which he completed only a few months before his death.

He will serve as an example of another aspect of College life. Its unusual concentration on the performing and visual arts, music, drama, painting, sculpture, ceramics, textile design and

172

173

174

manufacture gives it a singular cultural vitality. Music seems to be played all over the place, almost all the time, and sometimes rehearsals in the Hall can complicate a seminar in a nearby lecture room. The summer exhibitions of the Visual Arts department, of paintings, sculpture, textiles and ceramics are an unfailing source of pleasure. Some of these exhibitions are held in the College Gallery. For some years after it was completed in 1975, it was variously used as a meeting room, a lecture-hall and a book-store but, eventually, it was decided that it should be used for the purpose for which it was built, and it now houses the College's own collection of paintings, and an interesting, if eclectic collection, held on permanent loan from the St Gabriel's Trustees, as well as providing a venue for special exhibitions. But it is not large enough to accommodate all the summer shows, which are set up in rooms and corridors all over the College.

In recent years, the Gallery has been the scene of important exhibitions of works by former staff and students of the College, including Bridget Riley, herself now an Honorary Fellow of the College, Paul Drury and Robin Tanner. In 1987, an exhibition of early works of Graham Sutherland was held as part of London University's celebrations of its one hundred and fiftieth anniversary. This anniversary was also marked by a concert given in the Great Hall by the orchestra of the National Centre for Orchestral Studies. This had come into being in 1979, as a result of an enquiry sponsored by the Gulbenkian Foundation on the training of orchestral musicians. The Centre has been an independent institution, providing a one-year course in which accomplished executants play together as an orchestra under the direction of conductors and soloists of

175 Sir Michael Tippett,
with the NCOS Orchestra in
the Royal Festival Hall, after
a performance on 1 June
1988 of the *Mask of Time*.

176 The Freshers' Fair,
1988.

175

176

great distinction. For the first ten years of its existence – a new
life is planned for it in Bristol – the course led to the award of a
Goldsmiths' College diploma. Its director, Mr B. N. Tschaikov,
had his offices in College, and although the orchestra did much
of its work in Greenwich Borough Hall, it frequently played in
College and also on important University occasions.

Another independent institution with close links with
Goldsmiths' is the Laban Centre for Movement and Dance.
Founded by Rudolf von Laban and originally based at Addles-
ton in Surrey, it moved in 1973 to a site adjoining the College,
and after complicated negotiations with various ecclesiastical
bodies was permitted to convert the greater part of St James's,
Hatcham, into studios and rehearsal rooms. Laban was an
outstanding scholar, theorist and practitioner of modern dance

177 The crew of a third-year Drama Department video production in Parliament Square, 1988.

178 Students protesting outside the College against Government proposals for student loans, November 1988.

177

178

and his centre was to be the first institution in the UK to develop degree courses in dance, under the auspices of the CNAA. The activities of the centre add a graceful and pleasing element to cultural life at New Cross. Another unusual element is provided by the work of the Communications Department, whose courses combine a sociological and philosophical study of the media with practical work in television, radio, film and journalism.

There are, of course, as in all universities, a large number of societies, political and cultural, religious and athletic. They grow or decline as a result of the enthusiasm or otherwise of their members. Some of the most lively operate in the cultural area, for example, the Drama Society and the Art Film Society. But, at the time of writing, the club with the largest member-

179

180

181

179 The staircase at
Pentland House.

180 Tables laid in the Union
hall for the 1989 Football
Club dinner.

181 A mixed hockey team at
Newquay for the Exeter
Festival, 1989.

ship is the Rugby Union Club and it may be supposed that its
activities are more social and athletic than artistic. In fact,
from the very earliest days, the athletic and sporting clubs have
played a very major part in student life and were much encouraged by Loring and his colleagues. He would have been happy
to know that in 1988 the Association Football Club won the
London University League title and that the College's Cricket
XI won the University Knock-Out Cup in the previous year.
The Students' Union building itself is the scene of constant
entertainments and has an enormous bar, of which the annual
turnover is sometimes impressively large. There are other
social centres too; the halls of residence all have a flavour of
their own, and there are two houses near the College, occupied
by the Anglican and Roman Catholic chaplains, where a rather
quieter kind of social life flourishes.

The Union and its officers have, of course, been active and
assiduous in protecting the interests of students, and in
making their views known about college and public policies.
They have also, together with tutors, counsellors, chaplains

182 An art studio, 1989.

183 Members of the New Cross Theatre (NXT – the practical research facility of the College's Drama Department) playing in Brian Friel's *Translations* in the George Wood Theatre in April 1989.

182

183

and others, had what might be described as a pastoral job to do. It is known that many undergraduates are attracted to Gold-smiths' College simply because it is sited in an inner city area and not beneath the shadow of some great cathedral. But student life in an area like New Cross does present problems of its own, different from though not necessarily less taxing than those experienced in supposedly ivory towers, and here the Union provides valuable help and advice.

184 On 21 February 1984, Honorary Fellowships of the College were conferred on Lord Dainton, former chairman of the University Grants Committee and Prime Warden of the Goldsmiths' Company, and the Rt Hon Merlyn Rees MP, former Cabinet Minister and President of the Goldsmiths' College Students' Union 1940-1. In this picture, Lord Perry is shown welcoming Lord Dainton.

21 Finis Coronat Opus

185 Sir Charles Carter, twelfth Chairman of the College Delegacy 1984-8, first Chairman of the College Council 1988-, Founding Vice-Chancellor of the University of Lancaster.

On 9 December 1987, the Senate of the University of London resolved that Goldsmiths' College should be admitted as a School of the University on 1 August 1988. Thus was fulfilled the hope of the Worshipful Company of Goldsmiths that the College should become the University College of south-east London. Thus, also, was ended a prolonged period of uncertainty in the College, and an almost continuous series of discussions about its future, which had extended over many years.

The report of the Murray Enquiry, it will be remembered, recommended that Goldsmiths' should become an independent institution outside the University. This did not happen, but the College found itself increasingly impeded by some of the regulations under which it functioned as one of the last institutions with recognised teachers. It could not, for example, plan its own degree courses, to fit with its particular academic strengths, as the Schools do; indeed it was very limited in the range of degree courses it could teach for. The phasing out of the IRT system put the B Ed degree under particular threat and the College could not, of right, enjoy the services of professors: their Chairs had formally to be attached to Schools. Thus the Lewisham Professor, although he worked at Goldsmiths', was actually paid through Bedford College, and, so to speak, seconded from there.

These complications reached a crisis point in 1977-8, when a change in University regulations seemed likely to extinguish all science work at Goldsmiths'. On this occasion the University acted quickly to solve the problem, and the College, taking this as a good omen, formally renewed its application to become a School. Assured that the College would agree to a transfer to UGC funding if the application was granted, the Vice-Chancellor, Lord Annan, appointed a committee to consider it, and he and other members of this committee visited the College in the summer of 1979. The application was then referred to the University's Boards of Studies for their advice, and the Vice-Chancellor ruled that, in the meantime, no new professorial appointments should be made under the existing arrangements. Professor Craft's Chair therefore remained unfilled when he moved to Nottingham; and plans for a St Gabriel's Chair in Christian Studies, and another Goldsmiths' Company Chair in English, had to be dropped.

186 Part of an exhibition of Balkan peasant costume organised in the College Gallery by Diane Waller in 1985.

187 Mr W. McCall (right) with the Warden during his visit to the College on 16 February 1986.

188 Many of these buildings were demolished to make way for the new Library.

189 Professor Andrew Rutherford, eighth Warden of the College from 1984.

186

As it turned out, the College's new application could hardly have been made at a worse time. The University was confronting a major financial crisis and, having appointed a committee on academic organisation under Sir Peter Swinnerton-Dyer, Bt, the Vice-Chancellor of Cambridge University, to advise it on how best to survive, it could hardly be expected to welcome a new claimant on what was likely to be a considerably diminished UGC grant to the University itself. Indeed, the continued existence of some of the Schools was already in doubt, and, very shortly, an elaborate process of mergers would begin, such as that between Bedford and Royal Holloway Colleges. Goldsmiths', recognising that the times were inauspicious, decided not to press for an early decision on the constitutional issue, but again asked for amendments to some of the academic regulations by which it felt itself inhibited.

The first draft of the Vice-Chancellor's committee's report came as another shock. It bluntly recommended that the College should seek an independent future in the public sector, and that it should admit no students to read for London degrees from 1986 onwards. In fact, the final version of this report,

187

189

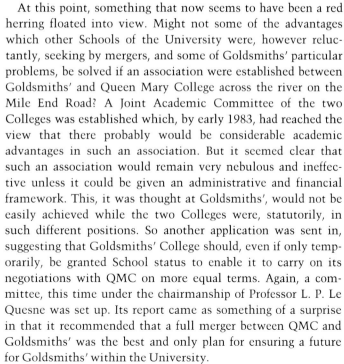

188

which appeared in the summer of 1982, was considerably less severe. It recognised the academic need to relax some of the regulations under which the College laboured; proposed new arrangements by which it could continue to teach for a B Ed degree; and expressed the view that the College and the University would have to work closely together in determining the College's future. Five years were left for the process to be completed, as the embargo on the admission of degree students was not lifted, only deferred for two years.

At this point, something that now seems to have been a red herring floated into view. Might not some of the advantages which other Schools of the University were, however reluctantly, seeking by mergers, and some of Goldsmiths' particular problems, be solved if an association were established between Goldsmiths' and Queen Mary College across the river on the Mile End Road? A Joint Academic Committee of the two Colleges was established which, by early 1983, had reached the view that there probably would be considerable academic advantages in such an association. But it seemed clear that such an association would remain very nebulous and ineffective unless it could be given an administrative and financial framework. This, it was thought at Goldsmiths', would not be easily achieved while the two Colleges were, statutorily, in such different positions. So another application was sent in, suggesting that Goldsmiths' College should, even if only temporarily, be granted School status to enable it to carry on its negotiations with QMC on more equal terms. Again, a committee, this time under the chairmanship of Professor L. P. Le Quesne was set up. Its report came as something of a surprise in that it recommended that a full merger between QMC and Goldsmiths' was the best and only plan for ensuring a future for Goldsmiths' within the University.

So for several months in 1984 and 1985 detailed discussions on financial and governmental matters took place between the

190 Lord Flowers,
Vice-Chancellor of the
University of London,
opening an exhibition of the
early works of Graham
Sutherland on 29 October
1986, which was held as part
of the 150th anniversary
celebrations of the
University. Lady Flowers
and the Warden are shown
on the right of the picture.

191 On 3 March 1987,
Honorary Fellowships were
conferred on Dr Richard
Hoggart, former Warden,
Miss Bridget Riley,
distinguished artist and
former student, Professor Sir
Randolph Quirk, former
Vice-Chancellor of the
University of London and
President of the British
Academy, and Vernon
Handley, distinguished
conductor.

190

191

two Colleges. One particularly memorable session was held in the gallery at Goldsmiths, where an exhibition of Balkan folk costumes happened to be on show. Huge white-faced plaster figures, robed in brilliant peasant dress, loomed over negotiators anxiously pondering the probable effects of Goldsmiths' College staff transferring to a different and more costly pension scheme. But in the event, these negotiations came to nothing, mainly because the financial future of a merged institution was too uncertain. From Goldsmiths' point of view, the urgency of arriving at a decision of some kind or other was now very great. The 1988 deadline was getting perilously close and, in May 1985, the Hon. Peter Brooke MP, Parliamentary Under-Secretary of State at the Department of Education and Science,

192   193

192 The new College flag
flew for the first time on 3
March 1987.

193 The Warden and Mrs
Rutherford had a narrow
escape on the night of the
great storm, 18 October
1987, when a massive
chimney crashed through
the roof above their bedroom
at Farnham House, the
Warden's official residence.

formally told the College that a decision must shortly be made.
Either it must move fully into the University sector, receive its
funds from the UGC by way of the Court of London University, and so come under the ultimate planning control of the
UGC, or it must move into the public sector and come under
the planning control of the National Advisory Body, whose
functions more or less paralleled those of the UGC.

In fact, exploratory talks about association or merger had
already taken place with Thames Polytechnic and Avery Hill
College, and with officials of the ILEA. But, when the University, having learnt of the failure of the QMC discussions, asked
the College for a detailed statement of the options it considered to be open to it, the answer was as before. It would
prefer to remain within the University, possibly in some form
of association with Birkbeck College – for another possible
liaison, if not marriage, had been mooted – even if School
status was unobtainable; only if that was ruled out would it
move, reluctantly, into the public sector and in that event
would prefer to retain its independence.

The Joint Planning Committee of the University, having
received a presentation of the College's case from the Warden,
then took a step which was to lead, just over two years later, to
the Senate Resolution of 9 December 1987. It set up a committee under the chairmanship of Mr W. McCall, a lay member
of the University Court, further comprising three representatives from Birkbeck College and three from Goldsmiths',
together with Professor R. A. Howie (Chairman of the Academic Council), Dr I. G. Patel (Director of the LSE), and
Professor S. R. Sutherland (Principal of King's College). Its
terms of reference were as follows:

1 To consider the case for an association between Goldsmiths'
   College and Birkbeck, and to advise on how such an
   association might operate;
2 To submit an initial appraisal of their task, together with a
   timetable, to the meeting of the JPC on 14 November 1985;
3 To examine, if necessary, such other possibilities relating to
   the future of Goldsmiths' College as the Working Group see
   fit;
4 To submit a report as soon as possible for consideration by the
   two Colleges and the JPC.

The third of these clauses was to prove to be of great
importance, for it fairly soon became clear to the Working Party
that no particular advantages would be secured by either a
formal association or an actual merger between Birkbeck and
Goldsmiths', and the third clause enabled the committee to
consider other possibilities.

Three points are worth making about the operations of this
committee. For the first time, representatives of Goldsmiths'
were actually members of a University committee charged with
considering its future; on previous occasions, the Warden had
appeared simply as a suppliant or, at best, a witness. Secondly,
the committee was determined to find early solutions, inspired,
perhaps, by the strongly expressed views of Sir Randolph Quirk
(Vice-Chancellor 1981-5) and Lord Flowers (Vice-Chancellor
from 1985) that the time had come for the College's future to be
decided. Thirdly, the committee considered not only the
validity of Goldsmiths' claims, but also asked itself whether
granting them would be of advantage not only to the College,
but to the University.

In its final report, it recommended that Goldsmiths' should
become a School of the University but that its future academic
work should take quite specific forms. It felt that the College's
experience and strength in adult and community education
would be of advantage to the University, and that it should
concentrate on courses which would be distinctive, and not
simply replicate those already offered in other Schools. To quote
its second recommendation: 'The College should have a distinctive role within the University as a provider of continuing
education and should concentrate in both its full-time and part-
time work on the subjects in which it has developed a high
reputation'. It quite explicitly recommended that science degree
teaching at Goldsmiths' should come to an end, as it saw no
reason to recommend any change in the University's agreed
policy that science teaching should be concentrated on a small
number of sites already determined.

The McCall Committee's Report was accepted in principle by
the University, but there were still some tricky stretches of

194 The new Library building came into use in the autumn of 1988.

Sinai to be traversed before the College could reach the promised land. The summer of 1986 was spent in preparing an academic plan (or profile, as a plan now tends to be called) to demonstrate to the Academic Council of the University that the College actually could, and would, meet the academic recommendations of the McCall Report. Then it had to convince itself and the University, that it could actually function as proposed on a progressively lower level of funding without going bankrupt or becoming a charge on University funds. It was not until the autumn of 1987 that, owing largely to the skills of the Finance Officer and the readiness of the College to accept draconian proposals for economies and, in particular, for staff reductions, that the financial way ahead was cleared. Finally, the UGC had to agree to accept Goldsmiths' as one of its clients. So, the College received another visitation, this time from the Vice-Chairman and three of his colleagues. Their report was favourable and Ministers agreed to the funding levels required. So, suddenly, in late November and early December 1987, the

195

mists cleared, the road opened up and the Senate made its
historic decision. And, happily, the Warden had not suffered the
fate of Moses. Rather, his elevation, or restoration, to a
professorial chair was the first fruit of the new dispensation.

Andrew Rutherford had succeeded Richard Hoggart in 1984.
Given what was to happen, it was perhaps appropriate that he
should have been the first Warden to have had an entirely
traditional kind of university career; undergraduate at Edin-
burgh, postgraduate student at Oxford, lecturer at Edinburgh
University, Regius Professor of English and Vice-Principal at
Aberdeen; distinguished Byron scholar and editor of Kipling. But
he took, if one may say so, to the much less orthodox world of
Goldsmiths' like a duck to water, and there are few in the
College, or the University, who doubt that the December 1987

196

decision owed a great deal to his resolute and courteous leadership, and complete mastery of what was often a highly confusing situation.

The saddest effect of that decision had been the continuing need to reduce staff and to close the Science Departments. There was an irony in the fact that, back in the early years, there had been science and engineering undergraduates before the College had even begun to teach for Arts degrees. But, on this matter, the McCall Committee's Report brooked no debate and a transfer of the Science Departments, and of the Rachel McMillan building in Deptford, to Thames Polytechnic was effected.

On 2 November 1988, Her Royal Highness, the Princess Royal, made an official visit to the College, the first by a Chancellor of London University since the Earl of Athlone's in 1947. She saw several departments at work, met a good number of staff and students and made her own pleasure at the upturn in the College's affairs pleasingly clear.

It was by a happy coincidence that the new Library actually came into use in October 1988. For many years, the College had been urging on the DES its need for such a building. The old library, inconveniently housed on the top floor of Shaw's building, had been inadequate in many respects. It had had to be reconstructed in a great hurry after its destruction during the war and suffered a further serious fire in 1971. It was, in size and layout, simply not up to scratch.

In 1983, a DES architect, auspiciously named Miss Lutyens, visited the College, and there followed a series of discussions about how big a new library ought to be and how large a subvention towards its costs the Government could provide. In the event, it was determined that the cost of the new building and of converting the old library to other purposes, would be about £3.4 million of which the Government would provide about £2.3 million. The College successfully raised its share of the total, partly from donations by private individuals, partly by gifts from a number of Trusts and Foundations, including one of £50,000 from the ever-generous Goldsmiths' Company. Even so, the College had to sell off one of its earliest Halls of Residence, Grove Hall in Blackheath, to keep its side of the bargain.

A small committee was appointed to choose an architect and, after visiting a number of recently built academic libraries, it offered the contract to a London-based firm called Castle Park Hook – it was shortly to rename itself Castle Park Hook Whitehead Stanway – with Mr David Whitehead as the partner chiefly responsible. Inside, the building is airy and commodious. In scale, a three-storey building under a pitched roof, and in texture, elegantly patterned brick, it sits harmoniously with nearby buildings, and would do so the more obviously, if the building line between it and Shaw's main front was not so crudely broken by the graceless bulk of the Warmington Tower. It is the sort of building of which one hopes that the Chancellor's august brother would approve.

The pace of development has not slackened since the College's admission as a School of the University. The many administrative tasks resulting from its new status occupied much time in the session 1988-89, with changes in the accounting systems, in pension schemes, in grades and salary scales, and in terms and conditions of employment. Many innovations in academic course provision have also been effected, with new School-based (as opposed to federal) degrees, which draw on the College's special strengths, coming into operation from October 1990, or in some cases from October 1991. The changed status of Goldsmiths' also allows for the first time for the appointment of suitable candidates to University of London Chairs and Readerships within the College; and it has got off to a flying start with the establishment of a Chair of Policy and Management in Education, largely funded by the Goldsmiths' Company, a Chair in Social Work, part-funded by the Wates Foundation, and a proposed Chair in Fine Art, endowed by the late Mrs Millard in memory of her husband, the former Principal of the School of Art. Chairs have also been established in English, Music, Mathematics, Psychology, Social Policy and Sociology, and others will follow as resources permit. The achievement of existing numbers of staff has also been recognised by appointments to Personal Chairs in Anthropology, Communications, Drama, Education, Music, Psychology, Sociology, and Social Science and Administration; and to

197 The Chancellor visited
the Television Studios on 2
November 1988.

Readerships (sometimes more than one per department) in
Anthropology, Communications, Drama, Education, English,
German, Fine Art, History, Mathematics, Music, Psychology,
Religious Studies, Social History and Social Science and Administration. Recognition of existing scholarly strength is
therefore going along with the strengthening of academic
leadership at the highest level by outside appointments.

A major upgrading of the College's computing facilities has
been set in train, with valuable assistance from King's College,
London, the University itself, and the Computer Board. A new
Goldsmiths' Society, subsuming the old Goldsmiths' College
Association, has been founded to enable former students and
staff to maintain contact with the College and each other. And
an exciting new development, still under negotiation as this
volume goes to press, is the projected extension of the New
Cross campus by the acquisition, from Lewisham Borough
Council, of the adjacent site associated with Deptford Town
Hall. This, if accomplished, will make possible the provision of
new custom-built teaching accommodation, halls of residence
and commercial outlets, bringing considerable benefits both to
the College and to the local community.

The legal and constitutional status of Goldsmiths' as a School
of the University of London has been established by a Royal
Charter with its accompanying Statutes, approved by Her
Majesty The Queen in Council on 1 November 1989 to take
effect from 1 January 1990. The Charter itself was presented to
the Warden in the presence of University and College representatives by HRH The Princess Royal as Chancellor at a ceremony
at Senate House on 19 June of the same year, and this may seem
an appropriate event with which to end the narrative of the first
hundred years of Goldsmiths' history.

154

198 The Chancellor
presented the College's
Royal Charter to the Warden
on 19 June 1990.

22 Coda

Educational institutions have a knack of developing in ways very different from those intended or expected by their founders. This, on the whole, was not the case with Goldsmiths' College, for its history is characterised by continuity as well as change. Four principles or purposes have shaped its activities for almost a century. Since 1905, it has been in the business of training teachers at a high level; from 1891, with only a brief interruption during the Second World War, it has provided ambitious programmes of adult and evening education and so done its best to meet the educational and social needs of the local community; its School of Art has functioned without a break since 1891, with neither Kaiser nor Führer being able to still its brushes or chisels; and the College has never lost its pride in its place within the University of London, a place happily regularised by its admission as a full School of the University. And, all through, it has benefited from frequent acts of generosity by the Worshipful Company of Goldsmiths.

One last thought. Good colleges can be created by their founders but they are sustained not only by their leaders, those whose portraits hang on their walls, but by the hundreds, even thousands of people, who work or who have worked within them; those who teach and those who are taught, those who keep the books and clean the corridors and hold the gates; those who buy the meat and those who carve it. Goldsmiths' has, in the words of an ancient prayer, been much blessed by the 'faithful life and work of all those who have loved and served this House in their several generations'.

Appendix A
Chairmen of the Goldsmiths' College Delegacy

1904-1919   Sir Edward Busk
1920-1924   Professor A. N. Whitehead
1924-1928   Dr Graham Wallas
1928-1931   Professor A. W. Reed
1931-1944   Major-General Sir Frederick Maurice
1944-1949   Sir Stanley Marchant
1949-1951   Mrs Mary Stocks
1951-1958   Sir John Lockwood
1958-1975   Professor E. H. Warmington
1975-1980   Professor Bryan Thwaites
1981-1984   Lord Perry of Walton
1984-1988   Sir Charles Carter

In 1988, Sir Charles Carter became Chairman of the new
Governing Body, the Goldsmiths' College Council.

Appendix B
Wardens of Goldsmiths' College

1905-1915   William Loring
1915-1919   Thomas Raymont (Acting Warden)
1919-1927   Thomas Raymont
1927-1950   Arthur Edis Dean CBE
1950-1953   Aubrey Joseph Price
1953   Clive Gardiner (Acting Warden)
1953-1974   Sir Ross Chesterman
1974-1975   Dr Francis Michael Glenn Willson
1975   Cyril Wallington Green (Acting Warden)
1976-1984   Dr Richard Hoggart
1984-   Professor Andrew Rutherford

Appendix C
Sources and
Acknowledgements

Most of the materials which the author has used for this history are to be found in the Library or other depositories in Goldsmiths' College; in the Lewisham Local History Centre; and in the Library of the Goldsmiths' Company. The author has also found useful material in *The Forge: The History of Goldsmiths' College 1905–1955*, ed. Dorothy Dymond, London, 1955.

The author is particularly grateful for the help given by
Mrs S. J. Boswell
Miss I. Kiley
Miss B. M. S. Rees
Professor A. Rutherford
Mrs W. N. Spooner

Others who have generously helped him include:
Mr D. Anteh
Dr D. Asso
Mr A. Bailey
Mr M. V. Barry
Mr P. A. Baynes
Mr D. Beasley
Mrs J. R. M. Beverton
Mrs M. Bradley
Sir Charles Carter
Sir Ross Chesterman
Mr J. A. Coleman
Mr R. A. Collinge
Mr D. R. Cooper
Mr F. W. Cooper

Mrs K. Coote
Mr E. H. Cox
Mr J. Coyle
Professor Maurice Craft
Mr P. F. Cresswell
Mr P. Davis
Mr N. de Ville
Mr C. V. Eyres
Mr I. H. Gaber
Professor S. Glasser
Mr C. W. Green
Mrs I. G. Gulland
Mr S. Guy
The late Mrs E. A. Haigh
Miss Susan Hare
Dr R. Hoggart
Miss W. Hyde
Mr W. Jones
Mr D. Jordan
Professor A. V. Kelly
Mr N. Kirby
Mr M. Knee
Mr S. J. Leedam
Ms C. Levey
The Staff at the Lewisham
    Local History Centre
Mrs M. M. Lomas
Mr A. J. A. Martin
Miss S. Meredith
Professor J. Nisbet
Miss M. Potter
Mr W. A. Prideaux
The Rt Hon Merlyn Rees MP
Mr N. B. Rhind
Miss D. Rimel
Miss C. M. Risley
Dr N. A. M. Rodger
Mr D. C. S. Rogers
Ms J. Sheridan

Mr P. K. Steel
Mr R. E. Swainson
Mr B. W. Tait
Mr and Mrs T. Tait
Mr M. J. Taylor
Mr J. B. Thompson
Mr S. A. J. Tottman
Mr G. G. Williams
Mrs K. M. E. Wood

Appendix D
Illustration Acknowledgements

The author believes that the College holds the copyright for the originals of most of the illustrations in this book and apologises if, in any case, this is not so.

He is grateful to the following institutions and individuals for permission to use illustrations as listed below:

Basil Beattie   140
Birkbeck College   100
Mrs J. M. Braunholz   31
Castle, Park, Hook, Whitehead, Stanway   195, 196
Professor Peter de Francia   136
A. E. Firth   139
The Worshipful Company of Goldsmiths   16, 19, 20, 21, 22, 23, 24, 25, 26, 28, 29
C. W. Green   122
Albert Irvin   142
Michael Kenny RA   143
Norman Kirby   120
The Laban Centre for Movement and Dance   173
Lewisham Local History Centre   1, 2, 3, 4, 7, 9, 11, 17, 40, 83, 128, 129
Dr V. Little   154
Senate House Library, University of London   27, 37, 97
A. J. A. Martin   76
The National Centre for Orchestral Studies   175
Nottingham University   80, 81, 82
The Rev Christopher Pritchard   168
Queen Mary College   84
Miss Claire Rogers   171
The St Gabriel's Trustees   71
The Students' Union of Goldsmiths' College   180, 181
The Master and Fellows of Trinity College, Cambridge   57
Ms Diane Waller   186
Miss Melanie Williams   144
Mrs K. M. E. Wood   152

Index of Persons

References in italic are to
illustration numbers